Robert Walser

Microscripts

Robert Walser
Microscripts

Translated from the German
and with an Introduction by Susan Bernofsky

Afterword by Walter Benjamin

Some Thoughts on Robert Walser by Maira Kalman

NEW DIRECTIONS / CHRISTINE BURGIN

This translation of a selection of texts from Robert Walser's *Das Gesamtwerk in 12 Bänden*
(Jubiläumskassette, 1978) and *Aus dem Bleistiftgebiet* contains every microscript of the original
2010 New Directions/Christine Burgin hardbound volume as well as four additional
microscripts for this paperback edition (*A Drive, Pencil Sketch, Recently my eyes,* and
The words I'd like to utter): all are published by arrangement with Suhrkamp Verlag.
This translation was supported by Pro Helvetia, Swiss Arts Council.

Microscripts is a co-publication by New Directions Publishing and the Christine Burgin Gallery.

Neue Zürcher Zeitung reproduced courtesy of *Neue Zürcher Zeitung* AG

Manufactured in China. New Directions Books are printed on acid-free paper.

First published as a New Directions/Christine Burgin paperback (NDP1245) in 2012
Published simultaneously in Canada by Penguin Books Canada Limited

Design and composition by Laura Lindgren

Library of Congress Cataloging-in-Publication Data
Walser, Robert, 1878–1956.
[Aus dem Bleistiftgebiet. English. Selections]
The microscripts / Robert Walser ; translated from the German and with
an introduction by Susan Bernofsky ; with an afterword by Walter Benjamin.
p. cm.
"This translation of a selection of Microscripts from Robert Walser's Aus
dem Bleistiftgebiet is published by arrangement with Suhrkamp Verlag."
ISBN 978-0-8112-2033-0
1. German literature—20th century—History and criticism.
I. Benjamin, Walter. II. Bernofsky, Susan. III. Title.
PT2647.A64A2 2012
833'.912—dc23   2012024305

New Directions Books are published for James Laughlin by
New Directions Publishing Corporation
80 Eighth Avenue, New York 10011

Christine Burgin books are published by
The Christine Burgin Gallery
239 West 18th Street, New York, New York 10011

3 5 7 9 10 8 6 4 2

Contents

Microscripts
translated by Susan Bernofsky

Herrn

Robert Walser

Bern

Elfenauweg 41/I

Secrets, Not Code: On Robert Walser's Microscripts

Susan Bernofsky

Robert Walser, one of high modernism's quirkiest, most mischievous storytellers, wrote many of his manuscripts in a shrunken-down form that remains enigmatic even a century later. These narrow strips of paper covered with tiny, antlike markings ranging in height from one to two millimeters, came to light only after their author's death in 1956. At first his literary executor, Carl Seelig, assumed that Walser had been writing secret code, a corollary of the schizophrenia with which he'd been diagnosed in 1929. Unsure what to make of these tiny texts, Seelig published a handful of them as enlarged facsimiles in the magazine *Du* with a note describing them as "undecipherable," and then put them away for safekeeping.[1]

Now that Walser's position in the modernist canon has been so firmly established, with his popularity continuing to rise, it is difficult to imagine how it might have been possible for the discovery of his posthumous papers to have attracted so little notice. But after spending the last twenty-three years of his life confined to a sanitarium, Walser had been largely forgotten. What's more, Carl Seelig was possessive of Walser's papers and refused to allow others access to them, even after receiving a letter from a young

Robert Walser in Berlin around 1907

doctoral student named Jochen Greven who had succeeded in transcribing one of the "undecipherable" texts reproduced in the magazine. Years later, Greven would become the editor of Walser's collected works.

The "microscripts" have now been painstakingly analyzed by scholars Werner Morlang and Bernhard Echte, who spent more than a decade laboring over the transcriptions of the 526 diminutive pages, and so we know they were the original drafts Walser would copy over in a fair hand before sending them off for publication. In many cases, though, the texts remained uncopied, a final resting ground for the stories they contained and a bleak reminder of the discouragement Walser faced during the final decade of his writing career: As his work became increasingly virtuosic and formally challenging, it became more and more difficult for him to find publishers willing to print it.

The writing that looked like secret code to Carl Seelig's eyes turned out to be a radically miniaturized *Kurrent* script, the form of handwriting favored in German-speaking countries until the mid-twentieth century, when it was replaced by a Latinate form similar to that used in English. *Kurrent* is medieval in its origins, all up-and-down slanting angles. It is a form of script better suited to compression than modern handwriting, though its graphic simplicity—an *e* is represented by a simple pair of vertical ticks like a quotation mark, an *s* by a mere slash—means that shrinking it down results in a dramatic loss of detail and comprehensibility.

The dimensions of the paper Walser used for his microscripts were diminutive as well. The trove of manuscripts discovered after his death contains, for example, a poem written on the back of someone's business card and a prose text nestled between the lines of an honorarium notice. Sometimes he used the pages of tear-off calendars, cutting them in half lengthwise before filling them with text, or else detached the cover of a penny dreadful so its blank underside could become his tabula rasa. At the larger end of the spectrum, he once got hold of a number of sheets of the 13 × 21.5 cm paper used for art prints. On twenty-four such pages he composed a novel.[2]

It isn't possible to just sit down and read a microscript. Morlang and Echte report that one doesn't so much read these tiny words as guess at what they might say and then verify the accuracy of the hypothesis. To produce their six-volume edition entitled *Aus dem Bleistiftgebiet* [From the Pencil Zone],[3] Morlang and Echte peered at the tiny pages through weak magnifiers called thread counters— higher levels of magnification proved unhelpful because of the loss of detail. They took turns scrutinizing each page, passing their transcriptions back and forth until they were satisfied that their renderings were as accurate as they could make them. Sometimes there were words that continued to resist their efforts, and so some of the texts contain lacunae. Because certain clusters of letters in Walser's miniaturized *Kurrent* wind up resembling entirely different combinations, the deciphering work required creative as well as critical leaps of faith. In one case, Morlang and Echte transcribed the word describing the long fingernails of a barbarian empress as *Königindernachtnägel* (Queen of the Night nails), only to discover at a later stage of revision that they'd misread—the proper transcription was *Klytämnestranägel* (Clytemnestra nails).

The best explanation we have for why Walser began to rely on this curious form of writing for the rough drafts of his texts comes from a long letter he wrote in 1927 to Max Rychner, editor of the journal *Neue Schweizer Rundschau*, including an extensive discussion of the microscript technique:

> *When I referred before to the concept* brouillon, *I was actually revealing to you an entire creative and life history, for you*

should know, sir, that approximately ten years ago I began to first shyly and reverentially sketch out in pencil everything I produced, which naturally imparted a sluggishness and slowness to the writing process that assumed practically colossal proportions. This pencil system, which is inseparable from a logically consistent, office-like copying system, has caused me real torments, but this torment taught me patience, such that I now have mastered the art of being patient.

[...] This pencil method has great meaning for me. The writer of these lines experienced a time when he hideously, frightfully hated his pen, I can't begin to tell you how sick of it he was; he became an outright idiot the moment he made the least use of it; and to free himself from this pen malaise he began to pencil-sketch, to scribble, fiddle about. With the aid of my pencil I was better able to play, to write; it seemed this revived my writerly enthusiasm. I can assure you (this all began in Berlin) I suffered a real breakdown in my hand on account of the pen, a sort of cramp from whose clutches I slowly, laboriously freed myself by means of the pencil. A swoon, a cramp, a stupor—these are always both physical and mental. So I experienced a period of disruption that was mirrored, as it were, in my handwriting and its disintegration, and when I copied out the texts from this pencil assignment, I learned again, like a little boy, to write.[4]

By his own account, then, Walser began writing in a tiny pencil script to combat a sort of writer's cramp. This cramp or block—which he identifies as having both physical and mental components—must have been especially distressing to a writer who prided himself on sprinting across the page as quickly as he could march down a country road, filling page after page with his copperplate script to produce a novel in a matter of weeks. The pride he'd always taken in the flamboyant elegance of his hand shows in the swooping flourishes of many of his early manuscripts and letters, and it was just this skill that made him so valuable a copyist whenever he sought work of this sort when funds were low. Moreover, Walser evidently took a craftsman's pleasure in the physicality of beautifully executed writing. In his first published book, *Fritz Kocher's Essays*, for example, all twenty sections are of the exact same length. It's clear, looking at Walser's early manuscripts, that he loved not just the inventive process of thinking up stories but also the pleasingly methodical work of turning a blank sheet of paper into a beautifully filigreed surface. His early handwriting was ornamental—calligraphic and painterly. He manipulated the pen with the same sort of artistry with which his brother Karl wielded a paintbrush.

And now this cramp, this burdensome hindrance, had interrupted the beautifully straightforward relationship between thought and mark, signifier and sign, rendering the erstwhile sprinter stumbling and hesitant. The hand that hurts is a wounded warrior, it cannot practice the fluent speed that for Walser was such a vital part of the experience of writing. His physical body was letting him down, breaking its promise to move as swiftly and courageously as his nimble mind.

And so he adopted a radical new approach to writing, abandoning the pen—with its long and therefore daunting calligraphic history—for the lowly pencil, an instrument for children. And by filling up page after page with crabbed writing so small it defied legibility, he broke radically from the aesthetic ideal of the elegantly inscribed page he had pursued for so long. In this completely new sort of aesthetic, the shape of an individual letter was no longer in danger of not passing muster—single letters in his new handwriting were often not even visible! Lower-case *n*'s began to resemble *e*'s, indistinguishable vertical ticks or scratches. The individuality

№ 727. Viertes Sonntagblatt.   Der Zürcher Zeitung 137. Jahrgang.   Sonntag, 7. Mai 1916

Neue Zürcher Zeitung

und
schweizerisches Handelsblatt

Täglich 3 Ausgaben

Abonnementspreise:

	Monat	2 Monate	3 Monate
Zürich bei d. Expedition mit Ablage abgeholt	2.50	6.00	
" durch die Austräger ins Haus gebracht	2.60	6.80	
Schweiz Bestellung beim Postbureau	2.60	6.50	
" mit Bezug einer Privatadresse (Streifband)	3.—	6.80	

Insertionspreise:

Die einspaltige Kolonelzeile oder deren Raum 25 Rp. für Anzeigen ausländischen Ursprungs 40 Rp. Reklamen Fr. 1.00 per Zeile.

Redaktion (Telephon 850) und Druckerei (Telephon 5782): Falkenstraße 11.
Administration (Telephon 5060) und Expedition (Telephon 1018) Gotthardstraße 10.
Annoncen-Abteilung (Telephon 2584): Theaterstr. 8/ Gotthardstr.

Zur Ausstellung alter Textilien im Landesmuseum.

J. H. Seit dem Bestehen des Schweizerischen Landesmuseums wurde dort stets von vielen Besucherinnen nach weiblichen Handarbeiten vergangener Zeiten Nachfrage gehalten. Zu wiederholten Malen bat die Direktion Versuche gemacht, Textilien im Museum auszustellen; aber aus großen Bedauern der Damen waren diese Objekte immer wieder verschwunden. Man hatte sie nieder in die Depots verborgen müssen, denn jedesmal erwies sich der Platz als zu klein, zu unglückig. Ohne Vitrinen verstauben sie, ohne richtige Plätz- und Lichtverhältnisse können sie nicht betrachtet werden.

[...]

Berliner Brief.

Leute, die immer vom Essen reden, beweisen eine gemeine Denkungsart. Im Friedenszeit! Jetzt, im Kriege, spricht sich der Berliner [...]

(Fortf. folgt.)

Feuilleton.

Das Kind.
Von Robert Walser.

In den Kinostücken spielt, ich sah, trat häufig ein Kind als Hauptperson auf. Irgendein beliebiges, hochbezahltes Kind spielte dort seinweise eine merklich große und ungewöhnlich denkbare Rolle. [...]

Schlenther. †

Er half den neuen Wege bauen,
Die Brücken in den Zeichland,
Als er mit Schmerz und Erbvertrauen
In seiner treubaren Treibe stand.

Er hatte diese Müdigkeite
Mit Nordens Dämmerungen bald,
Er war ein Mensch, war eine Freude
Nicht eine Hand, die Totes schrieb.

Er wachte uns Formelloses,
Rutwillig-Heitres, Burschloses
Und trat in keinen Bühlerzohn,
Das auch im Alter nicht gethönt.

[...]

Alfred Kerr (im „Tag")

of the letters vanished, the smallest unit available for inspection was the word, but even more important was the line. These lines crept across the page in a fuzz of majuscules and miniscules like lengths of the gray wool Walser used to darn his ancient socks. Flourish and difference gave way to sameness and regularity. There was something unambitious, reassuringly safe about this new form of writing. Looking at it, how could one judge whether it had been written poorly or well? Handwriting that couldn't even be read removed a degree of pressure from the writer, relieving him of the burden of being always, as he wrote, in the spotlight of his own critical judgment. And a form of writing which even he could scarcely observe aligned well with the ethos of the modestly miniature crucial to the work of this (in W. G. Sebald's words) "clairvoyant of the small."[5]

These obsessive rows crawling across page after tiny page like columns of ants achieved something else as well. These manuscripts now resembled nothing so much as a blurry or distant view of the neatly and monotonously printed columns of text on a newspaper page. They made the writing process uniform, mechanical. If Walser, the writing human, was fallible and weak, why should he not become a writing machine, moving as methodically across the page as his legs marching through a snowy landscape.

We still do not know with any certainty when Walser suffered the crisis that led him to develop his "pencil method." The earliest microscripts that survive date from 1924—the period when he was beginning to speak explicitly in his writing about feelings of defeat and symptoms of mental instability—but clearly he began his micrography much earlier. Exactly how much earlier is difficult

Robert Walser's story "Das Kind" ["The Child"] as it appeared in *Neue Zürcher Zeitung*, May 7, 1916

15

to determine. Walser's letter to Max Rychner contains contradictory information upon this score. On the one hand, he reports having begun his micrography approximately ten years before— that would be around 1917—but on the other he reports that "this all began in Berlin," a city where he lived between 1905 and 1913. In the landscape of Walser's oeuvre, 1905 and 1913 are worlds apart. His Berlin years—he was twenty-six when he moved there and thirty-four when he left—marked the early blossoming of his career with the publication of his three early novels *The Tanners*, *The Assistant* and *Jakob von Gunten*. This period is generally understood as a phase of great optimism and productivity in his life, but it ended with a downturn: he produced and published far less during the years 1909–1912. His return to Switzerland and his native Biel in 1913 was an admission of defeat, an acknowledgment that his literary career had begun to stagnate and he was no longer able to support himself in a major European metropolis. And so it is easy to associate his "crisis of the hand" with this period of dejection. Indeed, it is widely assumed that Walser began writing microscripts in the middle of the nineteen-teens, taking literally the date 1917 implied in his letter to Rychner.

I would argue, however, that Walser's casual estimate "approximately ten years ago" is much less reliable an account of the chronology than the concrete bit of information that his crisis began in Berlin. And we know that he was already experimenting with tiny writing in the first few years of the new century. Some of his letters to his sisters Fanny and Lisa from as early as 1902 were written in strikingly small handwriting on pieces of paper either cut or torn to size. One letter to Fanny dated Oct. 5, 1902, is written on paper folded to the size of a postcard, with a perfect rectangle of tiny writing neatly framed at its center. This small block of text—a mere two inches tall and two and three-quarters wide—contains 113 words. Another letter to Fanny dating from May 1904 is written in a large, loopy hand, but it has been torn from a larger page, and a fragment of an older text visible at one of the torn edges reveals letters in a minute script.

Early traces of Walser's micrography can be found even in his first novel, *The Tanners*, written in 1906. In this book, Walser describes a writing process for protagonist Simon Tanner that seems remarkably similar to his own pencil system:

> *Winter arrived. Simon, left up to his own devices, sat dressed in a coat, writing at the table in his small room. He didn't know what to do with all the time on his hands, and since his profession had accustomed him to writing, he now sat and wrote as if offhandedly, without forethought, on small strips of paper he'd cut to size with scissors.*[6]

This passage contains no mention of Simon's writing implement or the size of his script, but cutting up "small strips of paper [...] with scissors"[7] was an important feature of Walser's pencil system. Indeed, if a person plans to fill a sheet of paper with full-sized writing, it is difficult to imagine why he would first cut it up into strips. Once Simon sits down to start writing in this scene from *The Tanners*, he goes on to compose an essay eight and a half book pages in length, a piece of writing that would clearly fill a number of full-sized manuscript pages in "normal" script. So why would he cut up the paper before beginning to write? These tiny pages imply a tiny script. Walser describes a similar writing process in "Poetenleben" (Life of a Poet), an apparently autobiographical story published in a literary review in 1916: "Incidentally, to be sure, he seems to have begun quite early on to write poems on small strips of paper."[8]

How early is "quite early on"? It would seem that Walser had already begun experimenting with the micrography that would produce his pencil system even in the promising early years of his career and long before this tiny writing came to be associated with withdrawal, self-defense and defeat. At some point—we may never know when—he made the switch from pen to pencil. And some time during the nineteen-teens he began to draft every text he wrote in this form. He continued his micrography even after entering Waldau Sanitarium in Bern for psychological evaluation and treatment in 1929—this volume contains several of the texts he wrote there—and by one report even after his forcible transfer in 1933 to the closed asylum in Herisau where he was to spend his final years. If he did in fact keep writing in Herisau, however, this work has left no trace: not a single scrap of paper from those years has been preserved.

So why didn't anyone know about Walser's pencil method during his lifetime? Secrets are magical. Something kept from the public eye can become a talisman requiring secrecy to maintain its effectiveness. The manuscript illegible to anyone other than its author kept hidden the secret of a compositional process that had less strut and bravado about it than Walser might have preferred to display to the outside world. And perhaps once he had gotten into the habit of not talking about his writing system—for apparently no one who was close to him knew about it—he just continued this habit into the period of his hospitalization. Why tell the doctors? They might misunderstand, and after all, he'd begun writing in this way decades before, when he was still healthy. Or was he unhealthy already then, and this miniature script an early symptom? The possibility must have unsettled him. Best not to speak of it.

POSTSCRIPT

Like Robert Walser, Maira Kalman is fascinated by the secrets hidden beneath the surface of even the most ordinary objects. Her pictures beautifully capture the sense of mystery that surrounds this resolutely private author ("No one has the right to act as though he knew me"),[9] particularly in the picture that has been chosen as the cover image for this new paperback edition of *Microscripts*. What is inside the package wrapped in the newspaper announcing the author's death in the snow? The question will go forever unanswered. We are left with the intricacy of the wrapping itself, the carefully knotted linen ribbon, the not quite legible insignia on the blue button attached to it. Just as Kalman herself paints objects in such a way as to give an impression of almost infinite, constantly changing signification, Walser too shows us again and again that "We don't need to see anything out of the ordinary. We already see so much."[10]

The twenty-five stories in the first edition of *Microscripts* have now been augmented by an additional four, including "Pencil Sketch," in which Walser describes the "pencil method" by which all the stories in this collection were produced.

NOTES

1. Seelig introduced the microscripts published in *Du* with these words: "This undecipherable secret code of the writer's own invention which he employed in the 1920s and later at the beginning of his mental illness can only be interpreted as a fearful retreating from the public eye and a calligraphically enchanting camouflage he used to hide his thoughts from the public." Quoted in Werner Morlang, "Das eigentümliche Glück der Bleistiftmethode. Anmerkungen zu Walsers Mikrographie," *Robert Walser*, Pro Helvetia Dossier Literatur 3 (Zurich and Berne: Pro Helvetia/Zytglogge, 1984), 95.

2. *The Robber*, trans. Susan Bernofsky (Lincoln and London: Univ. of Nebraska Press, 2000).

3. Robert Walser, *Aus dem Bleistiftgebiet*, ed. Werner Morlang and Bernhard Echte, 6 vols. (Frankfurt am Main: Suhrkamp, 1985–2000).

4. Robert Walser, *Briefe*, ed. Jörg Schäfer with Robert Mächler (Frankfurt am Main: Suhrkamp, 1979), 300.

5. W. G. Sebald, "Introduction: 'Le Promeneur solitaire,'" trans. Jo Catling, in Robert Walser, *The Tanners*, trans. Susan Bernofsky (New York: New Directions, 2009), 12.

6. *The Tanners*, 105.

7. In German: "und zwar auf kleine Papierstreifen, die er sich mit der Schere zurechtgeschnitten hatte." Robert Walser, *Geschwister Tanner* (Frankfurt am Main: Suhrkamp, 1983), 113.

8. In German: "Nebenbei scheint er freilich schon sehr früh angefangen zu haben, auf kleine Streifen Papier Gedichte zu schreiben." Robert Walser, *Sämtliche Werke in Einzelausgaben* 6, ed. Jochen Greven (Frankfurt am Main: Suhrkamp, 1986), 122.

9. "Das Kind [III]," *Sämtliche Werke* 8, 78.

10. "A Little Ramble," translated by Tom Whalen, *Selected Stories of Robert Walser* (New York: Farrar, Straus & Giroux, 1982), 30.

Microscripts

MAI

16

Sonntag

16. Mai 1926   136—230

Radio

Yesterday I used a radio receiver for the first time. This was an agreeable way, I found, to be convinced that entertainment is available. You hear something that is far away, and the people producing these audible sounds are speaking, as it were, to everyone—in other words they are completely ignorant as to the number and characteristics of their listeners. Among other things, I heard the sports results from Berlin. The person announcing them to me had not an inkling of my listenership or even of my existence. I also heard Swiss-German poems being read, which in part I found exceptionally amusing. When a group of people listens to the radio, they naturally stop carrying on conversations. While they are occupied with listening, the art of companionship is, as it were, neglected a little. This is a quite proper, obvious consequence. I and the people sitting beside me heard a cello being played in England. There was something strange and marvelous about this.

It would be discourteous to fail to acknowledge straightaway the triumph of the spirit of technical innovation. How splendid it was to be enjoying piano music that came dancing up to me from a magical distance: the music seemed to possess a certain buoyant languor. And now today I find a director's position advertised in a well-established paper. Thinking back to how someone once, at an advanced hour of the evening, declared me an out-and-out success—a characterization that by no means struck me as flattering—

Microscript 337

25

I asked myself whether I oughtn't apply for the advertised position. A leadership post. How odd, the way details of your life from the distant past can suddenly occur to you, for example this minor incident pertaining to my status as a "successful person." And the way I leapt up at once from my seat that night to challenge the one who'd dished up that expression that struck me as so inappropriate. "You owe me an explanation," I shouted in his direction. He replied that he had merely wished to express that he considered me an extremely nice person. Hearing this response, I declared myself satisfied. As for the directorship, energy and adroitness are demanded of the pool of applicants. A solid general education, the advertisement said, is the main prerequisite. That I am occupying myself with the question of whether I possess a sufficient quantity of what is being required here does not particularly surprise me.

Several days ago, by the way, the daughter of a household situated in the best neighborhood in town asked me: "Would you like it if I were, in future, to address you as 'Röbi'?" This question was posed beside a garden gate, and I believed I was justified in replying in the affirmative. You have to understand, this directorial advertisement gives me pause, and you will further not find it for even a moment incomprehensible that I am secretly proud of this question that a member of the upper crust saw fit to address to me. That I listened to the radio for the first time yesterday fills me with a feeling of internationality, though this remark I've just made is, to be sure, anything but modest.

I am living here in a sort of hospital room and am using a newspaper to give support to the page on which I write this sketch.

WELT

μίζω. Διαβόητον γάρ σε οὐκ ἐν ταῖς Ἀθήναις
ὂν ἐκεῖνος πεποίηκεν.

ως ὅσον οὐ διὰ τῶν αὐτῶν ἑκάτεροι πείθουσιν,
εῖν. Πόσῳ δὲ ἀμείνους ἡμεῖς καὶ εὐσεβέστεραι.

ρόßtes Glück, denn Du bist dadurch nicht nur
Griechenland kennt man nun Deinen Namen.

del.

Sophisten und einer Hetäre ein großer Unter-
as anderer Überredungsmittel bedienen, aber
ler Gewinn. Und um wieviel sind wir an~

nsgabe von ALKIPHRONS HETÄRENBRIEFEN

TAG

8	9	10
DONNERSTAG	FREITAG	SAMSTAG

L   I

Pencil Sketch

No, one can't always be taking things into consideration. This morning I overheard this apparently sterling maxim. But did these words spring from the lips of a man of truly sterling character? This is something I cannot possibly at present know. "Of this no consideration can be taken," he opined, seated among persons eating breakfast. It goes without saying that I did not know this man. I just recognized him from having seen him fairly often, his face was familiar—a face none too friendly, it appeared to me. The visage of this individual expressing the view that consideration was out of the question did not particularly bespeak love, in fact it radiated lovelessness. No consideration, hmm? How very strange, how very curious! If everyone shared the opinion of the one uttering these words of wingéd wisdom, as it were, we would all find ourselves sitting smack in the middle of the most sterling inconsideration, which admittedly at times, that is, at certain moments and under certain conditions, can serve to promote the most lucrative transactions. To my mind, though, transactions equally advantageous—or even far better ones—can, generally speaking, be achieved by means of consideration. My thoughts on this topic, if I may, are as follows: Individuals should attempt to utilize themselves for the general good in such a way that others are neither harmed nor compromised. It is surely permissible to declare this a problem of extremely great significance whose

Microscript 39

solution bears a certain amount of belaboring by both the iso-
lated individual and the populace at large, provided one may truly
speak of culture or civilization, which almost certainly ought to
be allowed. So there are still—to this day, in other words—per-
sons, residents, citizens among us who believe themselves entitled
to proclaim that one cannot possibly take this or that into consid-
eration. And why not? I for my part find that a person takes on
the appearance of a pinhead the moment he declares consideration
in some direction or other impossible. I, on the other hand, find
it a dubiously large act of recklessness if any one of my country-
men, whoever he might be, should fail to face up unrelentingly
to the task of investigating whether he might not be capable,
in this or that regard, of identifying opportunities for showing
consideration. This, quite simply, is my national as well as pri-
vate opinion. It is further my opinion that one inconsideration
sows the next, which I can also formulate thus: if a person shows
you no consideration, you in turn must show him none, lest you
debase yourself.

Speaking now of another subject that will occupy me only
briefly, I announce that today I heard a woman who seemed to me
to possess an excellent disposition loudly praising and extolling
the colorful display in the shop windows, and at once it occurred
to me to believe that women in general are too readily inclined
to heap praise on this or that phenomenon. Possibly, though, the
habit of praising harbors a certain danger, namely the danger that
everything will always remain as it is, and nothing in society, a
country, etc., will ever develop. When a person praises, we must
assume him to be supremely satisfied with existing circumstances.
When for example a woman praises her husband, she is commit-
ting a great folly, for she gives him cause to be smug, which will
possibly lead him to behave inappropriately. What I mean is that if
I wish to exert influence—and women in their totality must surely

want to do so at least a little—then I shall do well to exercise caution with regard to lauding and appreciation. I feel that women have opportunity enough to engage in either so-called good or so-called bad politicking without having to set foot in a public tribunal.

If it is permitted, let me swiftly consider the following: there are individuals of the gentlemanly persuasion who seem to hold the belief that every remark, every address from their lips to the opposite sex must appear to these creatures the most pleasant and valuable thing in all the lovely wide world. Their comments, however, are not always seen as providential by these girls and women, as I remarked yesterday upon observing a lady— this being a title quotidianly granted to every female figure of relatively proper appearance—who seemed displeased by one of these courtesies just mentioned. Where flirtation is concerned, all manner of factors regarding time, mood, location, etc., must be taken into consideration, and a friendly glance sometimes signifies something much friendlier than the friendliest attempt at initiating conversation.

And if I may now offer something that concerns me personally, let me report that it occurred to me always first to commit my prose to paper in pencil before inking it into definitiveness as neatly as possible. For one day I found that it made me nervous to start right in with the pen; and for the sake of my peace of mind, I decided to avail myself of the pencil method, which admittedly involved a detour and increased labor. But since this labor looked to me like a pleasure, as it were, I felt it would make me healthy. A smile of satisfaction would creep into my soul each time, and also something like a smile of amicable self-derision, because I was permitted to observe myself going about my writing so painstakingly, so cautiously. Among other things, it seemed to me the pencil let me work more dreamily, peacefully, cozily, contemplatively;

I believed that the process I've just described would blossom into a peculiar form of happiness, and, just as I might have done with many of my attempts to communicate something to the public, let the present remarks be titled with the heading the reader will find above.

Swine

A person can be swinish in matters of love and might even succeed in justifying himself to a certain extent. In my opinion, various possibilities would appear to exist with regard to swinishness, etc. Someone might happen to look like a person who appears to be a swine, and all the while he is at bottom perhaps fairly upstanding. One can say with a rather large degree of certainty that men seem to possess a greater predisposition and talent for swinishness than women, who of course are now and then capable of achieving excellence in this regard. Without a doubt one can find tremendous swineliness in the amorous relations between, say, a man and another man. I belong to the faction of humanity willing to be convinced that men are more in need of love than are women, who often enough realize that when it comes to what goes by the name of love, they are by no means living high on the hog. Would it not be permissible to make so bold as to find it lovely when, for example, some lay-about lothario has a lady friend or, if you will, a goddess whom he worships and then, one day, makes the acquaintance of a young lad who pleases him because the boy's features and build remind him of the appearance, character, and conduct of his beloved? By the way, I consider renunciation in matters of love to be almost certainly at times a virtually marvelous thing, and yet I believe there are many who have no desire—or lack sufficient emotional or other fortitude—to share my opinion

Microscript 200

35

in this regard. Now and then it comes to pass that women fall in love with women in some manner or other. Whether these women are refined or rather the most utterly dainty and delicate swine appears to me a question scarcely requiring a response. Instances of delightfulness are always intrinsically beautiful, so to speak, and yet under the right circumstances they may be swinish as well, for what is humanly beautiful might, as it were, be too beautiful for human beings, for which reason people are glad to place beauty in proximity to pigpens, as one is no doubt justified in saying. To me and several others it is clear that the willful confusion of the beautiful with the bestial is, in a matter of speaking, fun. Now an undeniable imperative can indeed be found in attempts to ridicule what is beautiful, dear, and sweet—what is, in short, generally welcomed, for while pleasure does not in and of itself entail morality, which is certainly alarming, it appears to elicit satisfaction when contrasted either directly or indirectly with material of a moralizing nature. It can no doubt be assumed with no small justification that never being anything other than jolly and merry is well suited to compromise civilization. Does not the endlessly endearing drag us down? If morality itself can, as it were, be a bit swinish, no one will wish to undertake to deny that it is a useful, that is, a culture-promoting swine; if, however, immorality robes itself in nothing but grace and beauty, one is left feeling obliged to suspect that it will provoke distrust and a need to engage in cautionary measures on the part of society. As a matter of principle as well as whim, I am now hurling my recommendation onto the page: let precautions be taken to avoid untoward beauty and happiness on the part of the beautiful and happy, while also, with no less zeal, seeing to the avoidance of excessive deprivations on the part of the disgruntled.

No one can claim that he is not a swine.

Redaktion
der
Neuen Zürcher Zeitung

Zürich, den

Jaunts elegant in nature

Jaunts elegant in nature now lay in the past for this sorrowful man, who in the course of time might well have amassed quite respectable skills in crossing his arms and gazing pensively at the ground before him. His youth had been framed, as it were, by severe, naked, tall, blue, I mean to say joy-deficient, cliffs. He entered into turbulent, harsh circumstances that required he steel himself. Desires no doubt awoke in his breast, but he found it his duty to disregard them. He was constantly pondering how to earn his daily bread, which, being rare, was difficult to come by. He made the acquaintance of nights he was compelled to pass without sleeping. The deprivation following this man everywhere prompted the urge to distinguish himself to arise within him, and where entertainments were concerned, impressed on him the notion that life demanded he abjure them. Wishing to walk straight ahead, he would at once find some obstacle impeding him. As for friends, either he had none or they were avoiding him, for he appeared to possess few or no prospects for making something of himself. And so he befriended loneliness, which has been sought and desired by many whom loneliness did not consider worthy of notice. Among other things, he one day went to a place where there was little to be hoped for but, on the other hand, a great deal to lose, perhaps everything. On this occasion he was favored by fortune, which has its unpredictable whims but aids those who face head-on the

Microscript 9

39

laborious while shunning the easy, who manage to demand more of themselves than of others. From this point on, his steps bore him from one enterprise to the next, and within the confines of his career he beheld each experience or conquest being followed by another. A young, beautiful woman served him well by making a good impression on his arm, but nonetheless he remained a person incapable of emerging from his worries, for wherever he went he espied duties seeking his consideration and pleading with him to undertake them. Here I would appear to have completed the first section of my essay. Now I shall turn to his son or progeny, who inherited his mother's curls and his father's genuinely handsome facial features, but a certain precious entity—by which I mean the worrying—was not imparted to him. He was allowed to spend his days in a state of distraction, for this tender bud led a precious existence. Not for a moment do I doubt this, for I understand him, and, since this is the case, my pen can scarcely find the courage to depict him or sketch his portrait, this lad who sat in his room reading, at pains to consider himself happy. Only cautiously, apprehensively do I lay hands on him. May the image of him I am attempting to create resemble a wafting breeze, a sweet fragrance! It can well be believed that the building in which he lived was a marvelous edifice standing amid a splendid garden prettily composed, in an illusion-promoting manner, of meadows, trees and paths, fountains plashing in pavilions. Anyone strolling through this park was instantly ennobled and moved to indulge in lovely fantasies. A small lake or pond whose gentlenesses adorned the garden and whose gleam rendered it even quieter and more isolated was enlivened by swans with plumage that appeared to be singing. The air appeared to be the bride of the garden, and the garden its bridegroom, and leaves and flowers rejoiced when the precious one strolled up to join them and address a few words to these whispering entities who sent friendly glances all about. From time to time he undertook a boat ride on the water, or else sat for a while upon a shady bench, entering into relations with all sorts of thoughts that harmonized with the peacefulness of his surroundings; to their fleetingness he made no objection, as he did not begrudge them their freedom. In his hair the wind was playing. Even as a small child, lying in his cradle, he had possessed a certain worth. He would never grow old, this he sensed, for aging is linked to a diminishment of a person's attractive appearance, and it seemed he would not be permitted to forfeit his grace or give people who laid eyes on him cause to think of anything regrettable. His life's purpose lay in being graceful, in being overcome [......]. No one disapproved of him, for which reason he was forbidden to become something to which breath and a form belonged. Surrounded by company, he limited his activities to well-mannered comportment along with something that appears to have been both enlivening and distracting. Not being known was the lot that fell to his soul, which remained not quite grown-up. What people expected and almost found it appropriate to wish for, in light of his preciousness, came to pass. An illness took hold of him, and he let it bear him away until he departed.

If I am properly informed

If I am properly informed as to her circumstances, she was more modest than she appeared, for her appearance had something classically stern about it, a virtue she accompanied with a mild, indulgent way of thinking. She had promised her hand in marriage to an industrious but apparently somewhat flighty cobbler, a pledge that, while it was quite faithfully and honestly made, nevertheless did not appear to preclude her devoting her attentions to two rather curious and still relatively young individuals, each quite different from the other in matters of temperament, with whom she consorted in alternation, now visiting one in his chambers, now strolling about with the other in that spacious apartment known as the open air. Let me dub the one who was principally a homebody the Deeply Pensive Individual, while at the same time I resolve to give the other, who liked going for walks and relaxing in good company, the title Light of Heart. Opening her bosom to her own counsel, she told herself quite frankly that she felt drawn in equal measure to each, which was no doubt just how matters stood. And neither the one nor the other would ever have presumed he might imagine a ladyfriend with greater charms [...]

What a nice writer I ran into not long ago

What a nice writer I ran into not long ago. He's long been dead, by the way, for he wrote and lived around the year 1860, and his name will add nothing to this discussion, nor detract from it either, as I am speaking of one of those understandably numerous authors who have been thoroughly consigned to oblivion. The story he was telling gripped me from the start. His way of expressing himself pleased me greatly on account of its clarity. He allowed me to peer into the parlor of a woman who was already quietly beginning to approach a certain matronliness but was nonetheless still beautiful. I was able to picture her quite clearly. In her immediate vicinity lived a young girl [...]

The Songstress

Any grown person was permitted to enter an establishment in which one drank a glass of beer while listening to the offerings from the stage, a sort of podium modest in circumference. Most visitors lingered only temporarily, for a short while I mean, in this place of entertainment, which was lent a certain dignity by the figure of the impresario. He set the tone—composed in part of earthy humor, in part of businesslike gravity—and with steadfast mien observed the goings-on. A piano player accompanied the individual performances with appealing, if conventional, musical works, and the sounds to which he was giving life proved adequately suited to lending the dancers that measure of inspiration requisite to pursue a calling that elicited contentment and joviality on all sides. The mistress of the buffet, who kept handing over refreshments to the waitresses, was fulfilling her by no means insignificant function. Smoke from cigars and cigarettes insinuated its befogging odors throughout the neither overly wide nor overly narrow room, just as, perhaps, the aforementioned man in charge was introducing one of the ladies giving evidence of their artistic aspirations with the words: "Here, ladies and gentlemen, you behold Miss So-and-so, who escaped from the seraglio," humorously commending her to the favor and good-natured attentiveness of her audience. The phrase he employed drew some laughter, and then the dance began, a dance which, as soon as it was ended, was rewarded with applause that, if not tempestuous, was at least warm. All this time, people of all shadings were walking past the establishment out on the street, for it was situated in the heart of town. No doubt there were good, dutiful, hope-inspiring, obedient, solid, and amicable individuals among them. The ensemble was not lacking a jester or buffoon, and among its other members who were contributing what they could to the crowd's good cheer, it boasted a singer, a fetching creature in a multi-hued garment pouring out her heart in a song that evoked a mountainous something whose flowery etherealness one felt as one listened. One might almost find oneself capable of feeling justified to claim that each time she sang, it was to romantic effect. Her appearance, the gaze of her eyes, her posture and her song appeared to comprise an agreeable package, and as I pen the conclusion to this little sketch, let me pay tribute to this woman.

The Demanding Fellow

Delightful nooks and crannies there were, real boons for jaded eyes—and indeed one was compelled to perceive in the man with the voluminous coat and the narrow, cerebral face a cultured individual. Frequently he wore a suit of black velvet, around his neck a cravat emblematic of his discerning soul. His foot passed through alleyways that gleamed golden in the sunlight and at times appeared to him like out-and-out delicacies, much like fruits that delight the palate. Splendid was the way, for example, that interesting buildings which had played a role in history were mirrored in the still, color-suffused water of remote canals. This, as well as other things, struck him as lovely and charming enough to devour. Here and there a tree touched with its leaves the cheerfully plashing waves, with a daintiness that defied imitation. Churches stood before his eyes like tall, slender and yet also shapely women. He would have liked to encounter, if such a thing were even conceivable, the erector of one of these many edifices with their expressive power so very worthy of being seen—he would have liked to greet him reverentially. When it rained, he preferred sitting at home to going out, for which reason the sky whenever he was out walking was always nice and blue. Amenable to his sensibility was, among other things, the circumstance that the people walking on the street made on him a foreign and therefore congenial impression, while, to his great pleasure, he remained unknown to them: not one of these people brushing past him as they walked could possibly give offense.

In all these things, however, lay a sort of jadedness of which he was scarcely cognizant, since he lived, as they say, for the moment, and this lifestyle constituted a form of demandingness that was all the more demanding as it went almost unnoticed. To all these things we have mentioned a new acquaintance was now added that from the first moment struck him as worthy of being called marvelous. Looking like something straight out of antiquity, a young, classically beautiful woman stood at a ground-floor window, her head filled with anything but thoughts of this demanding fellow about to stride past, who was utterly unintentionally, that is to say involuntarily, on the brink of falling in love with her. He appeared to have found his ideal, which he had formerly been lacking, in this woman who had favored him with a smile, and not long afterward the two of them established a free union on the strength of no other affirmation but their own. He idolized her, bedecked her with precious robes and bejeweled her hands with ornaments, obeying his own demanding nature, which to be sure was a form of egotism, something like an unchristian act. In any case he was standing, as he found he had cause to confess, upon the pinnacle of the fulfillment of his desires. And yet for this individual who constantly longed for something out of the ordinary, the happiness he achieved was a sort of calamity, such that he gradually came to regret finding himself so abundantly satisfied.

All his longing, how he longed for it again!

Somewhere and somewhen

Somewhere and somewhen, in a region quite possibly furnished with all manner of agreeable sights and significant figures, there lived a peculiar girl—being at once beautiful and clever—who was capable both of making merry and of handling her income or assets in a thrifty, economical manner. Her figure was graceful, her conduct pleasing, and she managed to impart to her features a suitable, endearing measure of restraint that prompted her to speak in a simultaneously animated and circumspect way. Important personages came to call, impelled by the desire to make her acquaintance, and were visibly enchanted, for she received and entertained them willingly and so in good friendship. Her garden appeared, with regard to its well-tendedness and multiplicity of forms, to be a match for—or indeed even capable of surpassing—any other garden. The food that originated in her kitchen and found its place on the table seemed to have been exquisitely prepared and was in every sense delectable. Isn't it true that I am describing here a virtually fantastical person? Among the aforementioned guests who spent time with her so as to refresh themselves in mind and spirit and allow, in passing, their powers of understanding to experience a rejuvenation, there numbered at first a restless fellow who, unable to feel at ease anywhere at all, could not stand it here either and soon, that is, relatively swiftly, made himself scarce, should one be permitted to express oneself humoristically. A second gentleman was too outstanding for his tact to allow him to permit the above-mentioned lady to witness him lingering in her chambers longer than a scantily measured week, in the course of which, to be sure, he behaved in a downright exemplary fashion, by which I mean with man-of-the-world elegance. A third stood out by virtue of his stubborn, gnarly, practically all too stumpy and wooden personality: no early-morning dew, no tenderly melodious evening panorama could stir him. He was moved only by things that concerned him directly. A fourth one sat—pursuing his studies all day long without a single glance to spare for life and its sunninesses—in the chamber placed at his disposal by the gracious lady, where he read book after book until night arrived and the flickering of stars recalled to him the immensity of the universe, in the spirit of which he then immersed himself. There was still the one or the other of all these many men who could be mentioned, each hastening up in order to expand the circle of the eaters at her board, that is, to [...]. The best one of all this lady never saw, for which reason she found herself compelled just to think of him: "If only he too would come," she wished, but apparently he preferred to sojourn elsewhere, and only his heart remained with her.

The Train Station (II)

One of the cleverest and most practical technological advances brought forth by the modern age is, in my opinion, the train station. Daily, hourly, trains rush either into or out of it, bearing persons of all ages and characters and of every profession off into the distance or else whisking them back home. What a life pageant is offered by this entity I am reporting on here with pleasure, though also without describing it all too exhaustively, as I am not an expert. I hope I am justified in observing it instead from a more general, accessible angle. The very picture the station presents, with all its comings and goings, can be described as highly agreeable, and to this must be added all the particularly refreshing and delightful sounds—the shouts, people talking, the rolling of wheels, and the reverberation of hurrying footsteps. Here a little lady is selling newspapers, and over there packages and small valises are being checked at the baggage counter for such and such a length of time. Amid the graceful clinking of useful money, train tickets are being requested and dispensed. A person about to set off on a journey quickly partakes of a sausage or plate of soup in the restaurant to fortify himself. In the spacious waiting rooms, male and female possessors of wanderlust cool their heels, some with a pleasure-filled jaunt before them, others pursuing serious business objectives and mercantile or commercial plans aimed at preserving their subsistence. Books are on display and for sale at a kiosk, including merely entertaining or suspenseful volumes and high-quality reading material. You need only reach out your hand for culture and pay the specified price. Elsewhere you encounter fruits such as apples, pears, cherries and bananas. Posters inform you of the interesting sights to be seen all over the world, for example an ancient city, quays bearing palace hotels, a mountain peak, an imposing cathedral, or a palm-studded landscape with pyramids. All manner of things both known and unknown are parading by. I myself am sometimes well-known, sometimes a stranger. Often entire associations go marching respect-inducingly through the main hall, a space that exemplifies the Machine Age and embodies something international. It's almost romantic to think that in all these countries, be it in the sunlit daytime or at night, trains are indefatigably crossing back and forth. What a far-reaching network of civilization and culture this implies. Organizations that have been created and institutions that have been called into existence cannot simply be shrugged off. Everything I achieve and accomplish brings with it obligations. My activity is superior to me.

It's lovely when a parting takes place at a train station or else a reunion transpires and occurs.

RUDOLF MOSSE
VERLAGH

Herrn

Schriftsteller

Beiliegend erhalten Sie das

Mark

Crisis

That sometimes children at play can manage to be merry puts me in a critical frame of mind.

Could this sentence, which perhaps seems not the most jubilantly exultant where its framer's framework is concerned, merit criticism?

I wish I had the right to find fault with Herr Zigerli's claim pertaining to a crisis of cheerfulness that, in his opinion, is making itself felt within the confines of present-day human society.

May I be permitted to present the aforementioned gentleman to the reader as an educational advocate, a personality whose self-congratulatoriness regarding his leadership role is far from unequivocal?

After all, art and literature and all these other fine things—quick as they are to give the impression that they feel put-upon or out of sorts—have always in my opinion been, as it were, a bit crisis-prone.

Incidentally, the world-unweariness that can be discerned not only here and there but almost everywhere, using only relatively low levels, as it were, of observational zeal, allows me to ascertain a phenomenon on the one hand, while on the other appearing to be a fact that cannot preclude my recalling an individual of somewhat Sacher-Masoch-type leanings thanks to whose outright absence day after day from the premises where he resided along with his by no means unimpeachable qualities, I found myself tempted to pursue a not only critical but also, as goes without saying, merely occasional conversation with his wife.

Just as I was granting her leave not to forbid me to bring her warm and at the same time cold hand into contact with my lips—a gesture instigated with a nineteenth-century ardor that lent expression to a salonlike elegance—I heard this representative of femininity who was utterly venerated by the sum total of your humble servant say:

> My husband pursues multiple petticoateries
> leaving me alone but not at ease.
> Was my treatment of him too carefree
> and is that why he started betraying me?

She added in hushed tones: "Be discreet."

I promised her I would. When might an eloquent and yet all the same taciturn wordsmith ever have failed to keep his word?

LE PETIT LIVRE...

APRÈS LA TOURMENTE

-.25

So here was a book again

So here was a book again, and again I was introduced to a woman. I've acquired quite a few female acquaintances by reading, a pleasant method for expanding one's sphere of knowledge, though one can certainly, I admit, become lazy in this way. On the other hand, characters in books stand out better, I mean, more silhouettishly from one another, than do living figures, who, as they are alive and move about, tend to lack delineation. The one who is my subject here found herself, as the wife of a tradesman who trafficked in cattle, not just neglected but downright oppressed. No matter what she said, he knew better. Constantly he corrected her. If she knuckled under, he was bored. If, however, she displayed the least inclination to hold an opinion of her own, he found her out of line. Before her marriage, she'd taken an interest in the beautiful, i.e., art, and the good, by which I mean literature. Now, though, she began to contemplate vile and wicked things and did in fact set out one day in search of adventure, intending to become a rogue. Soon she succeeded in casting her spell on a dancer who became her admirer. He, however, was devoted to another as well, one whose neck was adorned with pearls of great worth. The cattle merchant's wife, who distinguished herself in the dance halls and cabarets by her mysterious behavior, attempted to win the friendship of the lady with the pearls, but this attempt ended in failure. Not long after, she took up with an individual who thought as little about

Microscript 54

57

[...] or the fulfillment of duties as the one previously mentioned. Both of them seemed used to filling in for real-life personages while pursuing their amusements. And anyone failing to show an interest in such pleasures might, in these circles, suffer certain refusements. The woman wedded to the tradesman soon assumed the name "the lady in green feathers." She called to mind a vision of springtime. But sweet and dear as she looked, her thoughts were hard, and she was set on using them to debauch these insolent debauchees. It was instinctual, this rough treatment of rough characters. As she sank, she dragged him down with her—all the way, in fact, to the bottom-most level of criminality, which is a sort of swamp. Along with her associate, she was brought to trial, where her testimony, calling forth an impression in every way splendid, delighted not only the judge but also the public that had assembled in great numbers. While the dancer and his colleague were sentenced to hard labor—admittedly regrettable—the blue-eyed, fabulously beautifully clothed damsel, who resembled a woefulness as she reposed within her own lovely being, found herself, on account of her justified innocence and to the joy of both herself and her defender, acquitted. When her husband heard the verdict, he too was relieved, as if he had never meant to cast her down, and now he lifted her up. Indignantly she thrust his hands away. Yet she was beholden to her lawyer, who sympathized with her. Thus does one go from happiness to unhappiness and then from unhappiness back to happiness again.

Herrn

Robert Walser,

Bern,

Luisenstr. 14/III.

Is it perhaps my immaturity

Is it perhaps my immaturity, my innocence or, to put it in a more ordinary way, my foolishness that has prompted me to ask myself whether I would like to enter into relations with you. On account of my total lack of life knowledge, I am called the Blue Page-Boy. And indeed I have not yet ever experienced anything worth mentioning except that now and then, i.e., relatively seldom, I glance into a little mirror. To you who asks me whether I might perhaps at some time or other, such as at nine in the morning, have kissed with my lips a little spoon that a woman had used for the purpose of eating, I reply with, as it were, self-possession, addressing you informally [...]

Microscript 408

61

The Prodigal Son

Once again I encountered the "incomparably uncanny man," whom I consider a likeable, useful person. Hurrying down an antiquated, perhaps downright uncanny alleyway, I bought tobacco in a little cigar shop. The shop owner insisted I address her as "Frau Doktor" in deference to her husband's rank. Courtesy isn't always quite so appealing but it does strengthen the one who, as it were, advocates for and pledges himself to it, who takes up its cause. The wind is comporting itself quietly; people are looking my way as if they expect something from me, and as calmly as you please I allow them to brush me with their eyes, whose beams polish, plane, round and flatten me. In my opinion it is one of the amenities of life to perceive the present as the eye of God, whereby I lay at your feet the assurance that a certain religious fervor prompts me to speak in such a way. This man of the world or pious man—which needn't be such an incommensurability—doesn't believe in "fat-ednesses," but now something entirely different has just occurred to me, namely the circumstance that imperious, dogmatic persons can just as suddenly turn into indulgent, docilely obliging ones. Repeating with great pleasure that I have a by no means unfavorable impression of this uncanny individual who haunts the nocturnal streets, I announce to you respectfully that I have now and then had occasion to see him standing before a shop window. He maintains apparently excellent relations with distinguished households and looks as though he were as old as the hills and in the bloom of youth—as though he were constantly remaining the self-same immediate middle, the good fellow who isn't good, the bad one who isn't bad. And is not, by the way, our very epoch itself possessed in so many respects of a quite canny uncanniness? But let me set this question aside for the time being so as to make my way swiftly and without hindrance to the "Glünggi." Even if the uncanny fellow may consider industrialists who read Ernst Zahn books and perhaps have even declared this Swiss author, their favorite producer of *belles lettres*, to be wobbly in questions of taste and matters of erudition, I shall nonetheless declare this spoonlet tale to be a factitious ludicrosity that cannot be thrown down from its pedestal. Uncanny Man is one of those everlasting saplings who, standing in a kitchen one morning at nine o'clock, press to their lips with indubitable enravishment a little teaspoon that a woman of perhaps forty summers has pressed into service for purposes of breakfasting. Are there not sins just as paltry as they are sweet? Are there not eyes in which contentment shimmers like a burgeoning summer? Are there not wintry dissatisfactions in life's warmer seasons? But devil take it, my Glünggi is still waiting to be dispatched.

I shall now come to speak of the famous biblical prodigal son, who sank with a beggarliness that knew no peer into the most pitiable remorsefulness, which would make him appear to deserve the designation "Glünggi" in every respect. This whimsical honorific refers to a milksop or oversensitive sissy, to whom apologies are of great concern. Glünggis are short on moxie. When they make a mistake, they sincerely regret it. At night these creatures emit highly resonant sighs. The prodigal son may well represent a prize example of this species, for he is depraved, and moreover considers himself depraved, thereby achieving the utmost pinnacle of Glüngginess. A different Old Testament figure represents the utter opposite of a Glünggi type. This figure is named Saul, and of him it is known that he had no patience for emotionality. Saul considered music, for example, to be harmful to one's health. First of all, he loved music with all his heart; secondly, however, he cursed its emotional capacity. By simultaneously drawing it to him and thrusting it away, he proved himself an inveterate music lover. The music pierced his heart, which, however, showed itself to be exceedingly, that is, most improperly, up at arms about this penetration. Once Saul let himself go. "Bring me David so he can sing me a song, the young wretch." This is what he ordered, and at once his command was carried out. David was not lacking in beauty and pliancy, and he was also the most peerless scoundrel. He sang and plucked the strings marvelously, with an outright scoundrelly charm. Saul, in thrall, but nonetheless enterprise-y and assault-ive, hurled his spear at the rouser and riler of souls. The boy was indeed riling and rousing petrifactions with his artistic culture. Saul was no Glünggi. Neither was David, for that matter, since he was taking no steps whatever to protect himself from hurled-spear eventualities.

Thus far I have lived through very little. One of the few amorous adventures experienced by your colossally humble servant transpired on an express-train and consisted of my falling to my knees before an extraordinarily well-calibrated voluptuosity in the form of a charming fellow traveler. On another occasion I idolized, while seated on a garden bench painted grass green and with a swiftness that filled me with astonishment, a lady who happened to walk past.

Uncanny Man, for whom you might perhaps be able to spare a shred of sympathy, belongs to the estimable clan or group of individuals who are unlucky to a tolerable extent and succeed in feeling happy about the circumstance that they are a sort of prodigal son. He is possessed of so-called healthy views. He is more innocuous than he suspects. He assumes he is merely uncanny, utterly failing to perceive his own cluelessness. Does this not bear witness to a pernicious kindness of heart? He has at his disposal a garden-variety erudition, which can just as easily be harmful as helpful. His immaculate overcoat is uncannily flattering.

The prodigal son turned up at home all covered in rags. And how unreservedly, how prostrately he repented! Uncanniness in our time seems to me possibly to lie in our unwillingness to repent, in our being too frail to disclose our own frailties. No one wants to be a Glünggi, least of all me. And yet I am all the same pleased to have spoken in this missive of the prodigal son. He met with understanding. Being happy, after all, surmounts and surpasses all frailty and strength. Happiness is the shakiest of things and yet also the most solid.

Usually I first put on a prose piece jacket

Usually I first put on a prose piece jacket, a sort of writer's smock, before venturing to begin with composition, but I'm in a rush right now, and besides, this is just a tiny little piece, a silly trifle featuring beer coasters as round as plates. Children were playing with them, and I watched them play. This game was unfolding in front of one of our restaurants, and a little dog had been enlisted in the little game. Oh, how his tail stood erect with pride as he found himself accorded equal rights. The dog appeared to be beside himself with joy, and the children noticed this too, and this silly doggish joy made them laugh. Then I too was made to laugh by the laughter of the children, and the little plates, these silly beer-glass mats, were filled with radiant joyousness at seeing themselves employed to playful end. Even these little mats could scarcely help thinking themselves in possession of equal rights when they went rolling across the ground with the same self-determination as the dog and children who ran to catch them, which was precisely what produced this happiness. Were these children by any chance unhappy? Not at all. Was the dog? The dog was silly, and being a silly dog, he was overjoyed, and it was nothing but happiness making his tail stick up like that, and as my own peculiar spirit witnessed this, it was so filled with glee I can't even express it, and the little mats, that rivaled the dog in silliness, oh how happy they were! I can't properly put it into words, and now the woman in the white blouse

Microscript 190

67

gazing down attentively from the silly, happy window at the little dog, the children, and the game with the little mats: a certain loneliness sank down majestically about her. All majesty must quite naturally have lonelinesses wafting about it. And now once more this foolishly happy tail with all its irresponsibilities. Gazing upon this sum of insouciance, misgivings arose in me as though these misgivennesses were the tails of dogs soaring up victoriously in pride, which by no means bears witness to a highly developed intelligence but nonetheless might apparently be proof of a certain innocuousness. Whenever this little dog snapped up one of the little rolling mats, it was taken from him at once, and the dog always expressed his gratitude at being relieved of his burden. And for an entire year I watched this game. An entire year? For a fib like this I shall have to beg forgiveness for an entire year, and this I shall do joyfully and with precision, even if I were to lose in this way an entire little yearlet of my life, after all I do possess a sufficient wealth of strength, prospects, sillinesses, and, I hope, clevernesses as well. And now these shoes on the delicate, voluptuously delectable feet of that, as it is surely permitted to say, genteel young lady decked out with maximal tastefulness who came trembling along at—let's be so clever as to say—an unsupervised age, swaying as she softly, softly walked. I gazed after this beautiful woman, this ideal of a lady, for perhaps four long years, and now because of this untruth I shall have to ramble about in exquisitely beautiful apologies for the next four years, a stroll I am certainly looking forward to, should this pleasure not be begrudged me. To contemplate a little foot for four years on end. What a great achievement! And these little feet appeared to be smiling at me, that is, perhaps it's more like this: It appeared to me that the little shoes were smiling, for how happy it must have made them to cling to the feet of so enchanting a creature. The children's game was dragging on endlessly, but "endlessness," you are lying, and now I shall have to spend an eternity begging and stammering for the indulgent granting of comprehensive comprehension on account of this lie, which I am only too glad to do, although it shall take rather a long time indeed, but I am patient and happy to suffer having all my snapped-up-nesses taken away from me again. The little mats were behaving in such a charmingly silly way as they trundled off. A little dog and children and respectabilities, and what shall I now receive in exchange for all these things? Please do respond at once. Might I add also that he—while she was sitting there reading newspapers—was obliged to tidy up the rooms she rented out? How awful it was, the way she kept waving him about, and he at once by no means misinterpreted each of her barely visible gestures, but rather seized and grasped them quite correctly, and for this, to add insult to injury, she hated him. I could write you a thirteen-hundred page, that is to say, a very fat book about this if I wanted, but at least for the time being I don't want to. Maybe later. Look forward to what might be coming, my friend, and until then, farewell. To conclude, however, let me quickly add one last thing. It would be such a shame if I were to fail to mention, at the last minute as it were, the fact that each time he had completed his work she doled out to him nothing more than a piece of dry bread. Her name was Rosalinde. He, however, was nameless. It would not have been fitting for him to have a name—this namelessness made him happy and thus he was provided for. The piece of bread always tasted fabulous to him, and when he was eating it, Amazonian rivers of faithfulness flooded through him. What a devotion that must have been! I know that you are namelessly grateful to me for these few lines. Oh these slice-of-bread affairs! Godful! I feel as if I could continue this report on into all incredulity... What else does the infinite consist of other than the incalculability of little dots? When she was handing him a piece of bread like that, she didn't even look at him but rather continued reading her newspaper undisturbed. She gave it to him utterly mechanically. That's what was so wonderful about it, the part that cannot be surpassed, the way she gave him the bread utterly, utterly mechanically. The mechanicalness of the gesture is what was so beautiful about it. I have also written this prose piece, I must confess, utterly mechanically, and I hope it will please you for this reason. I wish it pleases you so much it will make you tremble, that it will be, for you, in certain respects, a horrific piece of writing. I did not even groom myself properly in order to write it. This alone should suffice to prevent its being anything other than a masterpiece or, as we would no doubt rather say with forbearance, masterworklet. We wish to give forbearance the upper hand, and isn't it true that you were glad about the late addition of the piece of bread? I most certainly was. I would presuppose the greatest joyfulness on this score, for this is the most important thing, and you must consider it the best. You must without fail be satisfied with me, do you hear? Without fail. And then that little mat. This reality. This treasure trove of in-fact-having-occurred-nesses. This car drove off, and he and she were sitting in the back. How do you like my "trove" and "drove"? Make a note of these words! They're not my invention. How could such delicate expressions have originated with me? I just snapped them up and am now putting them to use. Don't you think my "trove" is *ben trovato*? Please do be so good as to think so. Accept my heartfelt greetings and do not forget the pride of that silly little dog. He was adorable.

M U

O Meliboee, deus nobis
Namque erit ille mihi se

Absconde te in otio; sed et ipsum otium absco

Hodiernus dies solidus est. Nemo ex illo quic
nemque divisus est.

O Melibous, ein Gott schuf u
Wahrlich, dieser wird stets N

Verbirg dich in deiner Muße; aber auch deine

Der heutige Tag war ganz mein. Niemand h
Lektüre teilten sich ganz in ihn.

1

SONNTAG / MAR

16	**17**	**18**	
MONTAG	DIENSTAG	MITTWOCH	

A   U   G

für den Beitrag

im Berliner Tageblatt.

N. 537 „Hochachtung".

Honorar-Verrechnungsstelle

Hochachtend

A Drive

Assuming I do not merely imagine this, one evening I carried a schoolchild into a house in my arms. A second little girl uttered the request: "Carry me too!"

Did there not once exist an illustrator by the name of Thumann, and was not, in his day, Meissonier a celebrity in the field of drawing? What ever became, for example, of Felix Dahn's epic life's work?

Meanwhile I experienced a drive which may or may not be of lasting value. Once a charming young lady went to see a jurist to ask that he shield her from a girlfriend's vengefulness.

While sojourning in a town that is by no means a major capital, I managed to sustain the pleasurable illusion that I found myself in a metropolis.

Constantly I discover as yet undesecrated corners within my being. One of my esteemed colleagues has written to me saying he has authored his way to ownership of a country estate.

Rather than embarking upon an outing on foot, I accepted a friendly offer to get into an automobile, and while I rode in it, masterworks of the current age went possibly unread. At a restrained speed I rolled along. My query to the driver of this vehicle—whether my smoking offended her—met with a courteously negative response.

Philistines are always fearful, regarding poets and their ilk, that they might be a bit "off their bean."

Microscripts 23 and 407

At one point I rode past a driver repairing his motor car, at another past a temple still under construction.

That drivers must be tolerant, placid, accommodating was demonstrated most delightfully in the course of this satisfactorily progressing drive.

The road led past rock formations and into a provincial town that saw me for eight years assiduously turning out and meticulously polishing prose pieces.

An elegant public square was tidily traversed. Girls out walking and gentlemen seated in cars gazed at me as at something like a personage who knows how to live.

Air brushed past my brow; from time to time a lurch or stop occurred that was transformed into new swiftness. Unhesitating journalese is surely not among my ample capabilities. I am not in error if at times I see myself as maladroit.

Roads appeared to rush toward me; a bridge seemed to me almost too narrow; in an industrial town a cinema came to my attention; there was nothing for me to do but sit still; behind me lay expanses of countryside, before me as well; now and then another traveler overtook me, only then to lag behind; at times the road appeared vaulted, like an arch; the car danced, flew, swam, played, laughed, skipped.

I believed myself entitled to draw suitable or unsuitable comparisons between slowness and speed, slipped—since I found the moment appropriate—a slim work of popular fiction from my portfolio or valise and then took from this publication, which was perhaps not without its charms, the following strange tale:

The village rooftops smiled; shimmering sunlight beamed flirtatiously down upon the inn, on whose doorstep loitered the daughter of the house. Quite possibly she'd been eating radishes, a few remnants of which perhaps lingered between her blindingly lovely teeth. Earlier it had been morning; later, evening gradually arrived. The sky had begun to resemble a richly embroidered little coat. Fir trees stood upon the slope; poets, who appeared simultaneously to be philosophers, composed five-act plays while reclining against the slender trunks. The moon's sickle appeared to be saying yes to life in every regard, something that proved too difficult for a schoolteacher racing from door to door with an illegitimate child in his arms, finding no agreement with himself. One of his pupils gaped in astonishment—quite comprehensibly, of course—to see this figure so long secretly revered now tearing about. At the inn, woodsmen and huntsmen played cards. Before a house that appeared to be remoteness itself stood a woman who, as you could see just by looking at her, had occurrences behind her, and before her she beheld a perhaps even richer panoply of experiences. Her very tended hair resembled a collection of short stories. While the by the way most kindhearted pedagogue still knew not what to do with his innocent burden, the child's mother, who looked on life in such a way as if the coming days were a toy trumpet to tootle on or a little drum to bang with sticks, lay in bed murmuring to herself: "Might he underestimate the irreplaceable?" The pastor said to the teacher, whom he encountered in their freedom of movement: "They are hard and at the same time must do battle with their own weaknesses." The child was heart-wrenchingly beautiful. The pastor's face, beaming with spirituality, possessed, as it were, something situation-restoring. In his spiritual alienation, the teacher hurled the babe, whose behavior called up no blame of any sort, willy-nilly at the pastor, a course of action that appeared to presume that the clergyman would now selflessly provide for the child's future. The existence of this village seemed to go back for centuries. In the schoolhouse, an evening of recitations followed soon hereafter.

When I had absorbed this literary commodity, a railway crossing barred my way. The driver and I waited patiently until the train had passed.

Fleetingly I thought of the plaint of the poet who had seen fit to write me that his life seemed to him like a word that had been uttered too often.

What I have succeeded in uttering troubles me not in the slightest, since anything I happen to write I soon zealously forget.

In this car I also flew past her, the woman I abandoned, which isn't even true, I just imagine it from time to time in order to suppose that she is thinking about me and that she and I together comprise a novel.

Neuartige K
Rand aus ro

Sie, an nicl
schönen K
Sommersonι
fleißige Pari
apéritifs.
  Die Vor-ϯ
Ihnen in Fr
ßen Flascheι
setzt, besteł
aus französi:
klarer, golɗ
anders als ɗ
italienischen
Modeschöpfɾ
eine neue F

Nr. 16 / 1293

My subject here is a victor

My subject here is a victor. Let me be thoughtful. I don't wish to boast. May my words be dipped one by one in a bath of deliberation until the language flowing from my pen abounds with a black velvet profundity. Not a syllable will be a fib. Among other things, I believe I am maintaining a distance from all jackboots and the like. What interests me here is a face, a figure, a human being, a destiny. 'Twas in the medieval period, when gunpowder was not yet in use. This era featured slender elegant castles and gaunt hawk-nosed ladies of rank with garments arising from the influences of antiquity. Farming and forging provided occupation. But I mustn't get caught up in details, instead let me plunge into my mighty plotline and grand subject as though taking flight upon pinions or wings. For the sake of a newly blossoming town, a battle took place upon a hill. I've stated this quite juicily, don't you think? What notion could have seized this hamlet, I mean town? Was it madness that made it believe it might be permitted to flourish and was required to prosper? They had begun to build a church towering up into the heavens. Indeed, their will to expand and enlarge was readily visible. The aristocracy was blocking the way, or else the aristocracy found in turn that this town was in some way impeding it. Now the victor shall burst forth with his, as it were, crackpot behavior. His station was that of count, and he had quite a grave and somber look about him, perhaps for the reason that his delightfully

Microscript 50

81

beautiful better half brought him only sorrows that he preferred
not to put a name to and instead kept carefully concealed. Was she
unfaithful to him? What an indelicate question! Did she dally with
him? O correctness, permit me to pass over this topic in delicate
silence. He was silent for hours on end. Each time he looked out
the window, the room in which he resided provided him, its inhab-
itant who dwelt within, the most charming view. But apparently
this view failed to satisfy him in any way. It was not pleasant sights
he longed for, on the contrary he felt a desire to be subjected to
trials. Day after day he felt most cultivatedly vexed. His nerves
were constantly summoning him to do something, to defend him-
self in some way or other. It was not for nothing that he wore a
beard indicative of manly intrepidness. Was his so stately figure to
wither unused? No, one like this belonged in the thick of things.
And so he took up position as a leader at the head of the town's
youth battalion in order to fight and be victorious in combat. Vic-
torious manuscript that is occupying me this day, go fluttering off
in search of acclaim: I too am a sort of victor here, this is clear to
me. Quite comprehensibly, the aristocracy now hated this crank of
a peer who had dared throw in his lot with the other faction. In one
of their assemblies held in a magnificent ballroom, they dubbed
him—in the course of the deliberations in which they were com-
munally engaged—a *Cheib*, this being an expression derived from
Arabic that corresponds approximately to the notion "impertinent
individual." Those who formerly had counted and depended on
him, whom he now had left in the lurch for the benefit of their
adversaries, ostracized and spurned him, and the ones he was aid-
ing, helping them out of their tight spot, merely shrugged their
shoulders at his success, which seemed to them at once desirable
and inappropriate. Cursed by the aristocracy and dropped by a
town eager to keep up appearances, he wrapped himself up in his
cloak, buried his head in his hands, and felt ashamed. In vain did

they wait for him at home. No one ever saw him again. Reviled by all, he vanished from sight. A later educator, to be sure, moved by gratitude, erected a monument to him at a suitable juncture. A plume billowing down from the helmet adorns the iron figure that represents the idea that took hold of him, prompting him to disregard his material rights—an idea that exploits its originator's contemporaries and only among their descendants can be accorded recognition.

A will to shake that refined individual

A will to shake that refined individual, to rattle him about as if he were a scraggly tree bearing only isolated jittery leaves, seems to be stirring within me. The wife of the refined and mentally exceedingly proper person one day shouted from their apartment window: "Passersby down below there in the street, stand by me and come to my aid, protect me from the inability of my husband, who is a refined individual, not to nonetheless brutalize me in every way!" O wife of such a husband, and O husband of such a wife, and O you millions of perturbations! You hordes of directors, come this way and display your managerial talents! But let us return to the refined man, whom I can't help imagining standing shivering before me, since, after all, considering what a sizeable number of writers there are, all sorts of people living today have grounds to tremble at the prospect of serving as models and being forced without their knowledge to kindly provide entertainment. With a gruffness verging on the invidious I go to work on him. "Catch!" I say to his horrified face, watching a spectacular iridescent pallor flit across the despondencies my conduct has provoked. "I think," he stutters in his horror at finding himself latched onto, "that I am relatively well suited to being seized hold of and ruthlessly tested." "Do you now?" is the reply I give: " So you admit it?" adding: "A discourteous person such as myself is as like as not to box your ears. Tell me, how were you once designated in former

Microscript 215

85

days by a splendid woman?" "She said something very unrefined." "And what was this thing it pleased her to utter?" "She called me a wretch, to which I saw fit to respond that I considered myself a person in some way deserving of such a vehement appellation, and thereupon this excellent creature burst into tears." People who are refined visit other refined people and confide in them, chattering and babbling out precisely what they have experienced and whether they found the experience indigestible or pleasing.

He numbered, as might well have been true

He numbered, as might well have been true of many others, among the good. Perhaps it is an error to go about considering oneself good with no further ado. One might naturally also refer to him as a refined individual, since all good people believe they are very refined, and because all beautiful people are virtually incapable of relinquishing the illusion that they are good. Once he founded a sort of enterprise, counting on the support of all the other nice, good, devout, joyous refined persons. Was there not a certain recklessness in this sort of calculation? Be that as it may, these good people left him utterly in the lurch, and the completeness with which they abandoned him might appear in itself to possess great worth. The good man was, at some point or other, good enough not to attribute particularly much importance to a beautiful woman. Moreover, this good fellow had brown hair, and when he began to think of something, his train of thought was brown. His blood was of the brownest brown. With his doe eyes he gazed—as one might possibly be permitted to say—in headwaiter fashion, perusing some Vienna Choir heights that can scarcely have existed, where the most stalwart acts of laziness were being performed. This Mr. Brown in his brown tailcoat was in the habit of meeting up now and again with a fellow dressed in black from head to toe, and the two of them could not abide one another. Mrs. Black consisted entirely of inflammation. Her calf muscles displayed a marvelous moderateness. From time to time she would inquire: "Do you two belong to me?"—a question that the stockinged incomparablenesses replied to with a cheerful, unambiguous "Yes!" Mrs.

Brown hated Mrs. Black because she harmonized too well with her. With artistic perfection, black and brown mourned a lostness that was re-found however in a person consisting of a rascal clad in sky blue who smiled in yellow, cast down his eyes in fiery red, and spoke a deep green. In contrast to the Good Man, this blue knave appeared to be wickedness personified. The rascal's blueness appeared to both the black and brown fellows to possess a historiographical beauty. "Unclothe yourself, why don't you, for you are surely in your nakedness a scoundrel of pulchritude, and you should know that we are Greeks in our thirst for beauty and literary cruelty. Seeing as the esteemédnesses known as our wives are constantly pulling faces at us, as the expression goes, we should like to indulge thoroughly, voluptuously, in rapturous appreciation of your person." Once they had made this valiant and honest confession, a wingéd, colorfully adorned monstrosity suddenly stood there before them. Understandably, they were horrified at the sight of this figure and wished to have nothing at all to do with it. This is certainly a peculiar story, and in any case it has never before appeared in print.

Im Auftrage des Autors ergebenst überreicht

vom

PAUL-ZSOLNAY-VERLAG

Wien IV., Prinz-Eugenstraße 30.

Journey to a Small Town

It seems that to this day a robust quantity of inexhaustibilities resides within my person. Embarking with more or less resoluteness upon this small town description, I shall allow myself to note how often respected widows with sons and daughters can be met with in small towns, and that, should one go marching from the train station into a modest urban landscape of this sort, one might easily pass by a park adorned with a monument to a bard enswathed in poeticalities.

Every domestic surrounding is at the same time foreign, since each of its locals becomes a settler or foreigner the moment he sets about establishing himself as a local in the homeland of strangers. A homeland is foreign territory for a foreigner. But begone, all you pensivenesses! And you, extensivenesses, please join me in their place. Buildings with arcades from the waning sixteenth and waxing seventeenth centuries, for example. As before, here too I have no desire to delve into geographical and seasonal indicators, I'd rather turn my attention to sausages and castles.

After a long period of motionlessness, I took a train again yesterday. Just purchasing my ticket at the ticket window gave me satisfaction. With extraordinary pleasure I vaulted into the express train.

Seeing as this prose piece of mine is looking likely to prove respectable, that is, mediocre, I shall entrust myself to it. I number

Microscript 116

91

among the sort of stalwart and enterprising persons known as activists, for whom there is no more gaiety-awakening sight than the one offered involuntarily by the timid and hesitant. The small town I am currently summoning up in my imagination, and which I had the opportunity to gaze upon in person, possessed a charmingly situated, architecturally most agreeable casino. Entering the castle, I visited, after paying a fee, a hall of knights filled with objects of interest. O you most splendid, most marvel- or miraculous of views that I enjoyed from these heights, let me not fail to devote to you at the very least, should your landscape lips grant me permission, a fleeting line. The glistening and firm rotundity of the sausages sojourning in the window of a pig butcher's shop won me over absolutely. In yet another display featuring goods of all sorts, chocolates and cheeses carefully wrapped up in silver paper lay side by side in peaceful communion. This information may prompt some reader to shrug his shoulders, while another one will be in no way dissuaded from continuing his perusal. As for the rest, the manufacturer of the present note sometimes finds his life work—which consists in constantly convincing both his contemporaries and the contemporary age that when he engages in his writerly vocation, he does so truly and fully, without bluffing or blathering—utterly dull, wearisome and thankless enough, and at such times he cries out: "How I envy those who are not obliged to be amusing!"

For some time now I have intentionally—that is, instinctively—been neglecting so-called elegancy with regard to my manner of writing and thinking, so that it might, conserved, remain available for my use, since the finer things are particularly swift to wear out.

I now rush headlong into the house of a small-town merchant to partake of four o'clock tea, all the while behaving in a polite, well-mannered and good-natured way, as though I'd never been anything other than an upright, reliable, skillful, serviceable inhabitant of the district. Let me emphasize in passing that during my journey to this town I caught sight of a European whose Europeanness I was able to ascertain only thanks to his, as it were, comfortably effervescent eloquence. He was dressed like an ordinary, by which I mean an unambitious, individual. Well, after all, a small town can lie just as well and unmistakably within Europe as any large or larger one. Now and then I make myself tremble, for in fact I've already demonstrated rather too often that I am capable of this or that, but now, recalling to mind my visit to that castle, I shall turn to the Middle Ages with my remarks. Given the inadequacy of my knowledge of history, I declare this in subdued tones:

A medieval castle like this moves me as if it were the visage of a beautiful girl. Fortified castles were constructed not out of pride but for the sake of their utility. Once, many years ago already, I stood before the gravestone of a countess. I bring this up so as to evade, for the time being, the difficulties towering before me. How cheerful I am made by a castle with its battlements and eyelashes that gaze at me as if it had large, speaking eyes. I shall certainly be addressing shortly or directly, and with all my heart, the no doubt inherently feudal phenomenon of lady's-shoe-heelism. In the merchant's home I mastered the salon tone, as I believe myself entitled to assume, swimmingly. But now let me take a running leap into the Age of Chivalry, inasmuch as it is evident to me that around the time when most of the medieval castles were being erected, Venice may perhaps have been the preeminent city to be found far and wide. Worms, Ravenna, Byzantium appear to be further noteworthy city names relevant to my topic. The question presents itself: what did life look like in the social circles of that time? Numerous cities that today are great were perhaps not yet even standing and thus excelled in their total absence of a presence, as they had not yet been founded. Immensely wealthy gentlemen would appear to have exercised great influence in that period, gentlemen of a splendid, grandiose sort such as one can scarcely even imagine in our jaded age, rulers who never under any circumstances whatever had anything salonlike (and I mean this in the literary sense) about them, a pronouncement or assumption in which I might be mistaken of course, since the entire modern world of letters is assuredly based on quite venerable traditions—veritable lords at any rate, without pretensions of politeness. Further, I am absorbed by the surely in itself not uninteresting question of what, in those days—whether at home or on journeys by land or water, in tents or aboard ships—was eaten: roasts or stews? What might have been the nature of the daily bread? With respect to sartorial habits, we can refer to existing informational attestations. The questionable question now suggests itself to me: What mode of speaking was favored by, for example, castle ladies in this era? Did they speak a language as curly as locks of hair, tousled and nonetheless well-rooted and as gracefully arranged as a covey of quail and as dark as the interior of a vast woodland? Shoes appear to have possessed, for a time, a beaklike shape, which we judicious contemporaries would graciously reject. It seems to me that in small towns the girls are more girlish, toys more toyish, and performances at the theater more theatrical than elsewhere.

I attended a play that looked and sounded as if it had been written during the Sturm und Drang period, thus dating from the Age of Genius when poets still displayed undeniably poetic countenances and devoted themselves to the magic spells of their profession more unconditionally and completely, with a purer, more mature fervor than may well be the case with today's poets. If I am not mistaken, the title of this poetic work was *The Rivals*. And should I happen to possess even the flimsiest knowledge of the theatrical arts, this performance deserved the rating "magnificent," shining in silky velvets in the costume department and in part trotting along on horseback. Admittedly, the play was lacking in glamorous female roles, but compensated with its abundance of stalwart, doughty, valiant, yeomanly, purposeful men. And all present found the heroine, a housewifely personage of exceptional gentility, refreshing thanks to her solidity, by which I mean her pliant steadfastness and her unswerving talent for accommodation. An intelligent pointy-bearded fellow took harsh action against a shaggy-bearded one whose trump card was his physical vitality, and did so without any more substantial grounds than the former's envy of the latter. He hated him because he esteemed him, and he persecuted him because it appeared the favorable impression that the one thus persecuted made on his persecutor would have to have its consequences. When at last the score had been settled, leaving the challenger lying vanquished on the ground and the conqueror of subjugators arriving jubilantly home, beaming with happiness, where his better half awaited him, she confessed to him that she had grave qualms about his happiness and was afraid for him. Our freedom hero blanched, deeply cognizant at once that his wife had given appropriate expression to something quite true. And indeed heroes prefer to see themselves in a state of struggle—pursuing their work, when that which they are striving for has not yet been accomplished—than on the pinnacle of goal-achievédness, where they feel anything but comfortable. In the abovementioned merchant's residence I witnessed an episode one might almost describe with a certain glee as dramatic. The merchant, you see, had employed two women for what appeared to have been rather a long time now: a housekeeper and a manager for his shop. The first was pretty; the second stood out more by her efficiency than her physical assets. On the day I paid my visit to the town, the directress of commercial interests informed the directress of household affairs that she had long been meaning to give her something to think about, a statement accompanied by an ear-boxing gesture. The master of the house was dragged into this womanly affair. "Don't work yourself up," he commanded the beautiful one, thinking to himself that beauty requires a bit of ordering-about. "I hope you will succeed in controlling yourself," he then shrewdly addressed the other. Finding themselves so casually reprimanded, while at the same time encouraged by such cheerfully conciliatory words, the two adversaries appeared satisfied with one another once more.

(Anzeige)

Das neuze

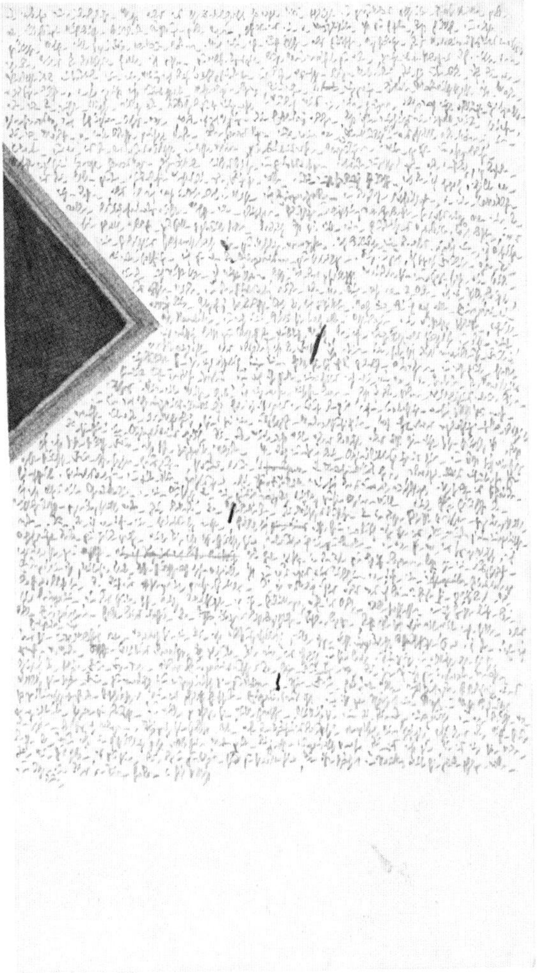

The Marriage Proposal

Just as indisputably as there can be both straightforward and elaborate—in other words sumptuous—prose pieces, it would appear to me that possibilities may exist for there being no dearth of both comely and unattractive individuals, that is to say, women. Yesterday I engaged a more uncomely than pulchritudinous member of the solicitude-requiring faction of the collectivity of humanity—at what hour of day need scarcely be divulged—in a suitable location, that is to say amidst the city's hustle or bustle, in a to my mind appropriate conversation, which touched, among other things, on the, as I am surely justified in asserting, most certainly not uninteresting topic of astrology, a science which, to underscore this in passing, is currently all the rage. Not long ago a youthful, i.e., by no means unelderly, fellow presented to me his horoscope with an as it were bashful gesture, which prompts me to make, with pleasure, the no doubt readily comprehensible declaration that I for my part would never dream of presenting a companion, even the most trustworthy one, with horoscopes that might be prepared for me by a connoisseur of the stars.

In my certainly far from authoritative opinion, horoscopes are either useful or harmful as the dear providences permit, who strike me as in and of themselves worthy of veneration. The not particularly attractive woman I was speaking to had received several years ago in a little restaurant filled with a colorful assortment

Microscript 434

99

of people—and at a juncture when I had not yet begun to occupy myself in any way with the obligations of Europeanness and the like—a proposal of marriage that was to be sure only fleetingly and heedlessly brought forth by the author of this present attempt at delving into the quotidian, an offer she saw fit to flat out refuse by bursting into uproarious laughter at my all the same cordial proposal, producing a sound that for propriety's sake imprinted itself on my memory. In those days, as I recall, I harbored no hope at all of being able to partake of European responsibilities. At the time I uttered the words: "Miss, to put it concisely..." "I know, I know, please be so good as to desist," she responded, and now yesterday here were the two of us seated side by side after such-and-such an interval, devoting not a single syllable to what had transpired between us. To this day I remain, my Europeanism notwithstanding, a sort of romantic, and yet still she seems to me, leaving all astrology aside, an exceptionally undelving, good-natured female who is more homely than particularly pretty. This horoscope damsel always imagined herself to be out of the ordinary; always she considered herself some sort of exception, and even today she is deeply immersed in this error, as even to this day I find myself mired in the errors of Romanticism. Only with great effort did I succeed in more or less convincing myself that I was born to be a man of reality, and only by overcoming hurdles did she in turn manage the perception that she was a fashion enthusiast. Although she isn't so pretty, she does love clothes. For not terribly pretty women to dress without particular care cannot possibly stand as proof of exceptionality, and for particularly pretty women to attend with great precision to their toilettes scarcely stems from a lack of originality, although both may at times seem so. The one I proposed marriage to some years ago doesn't consider herself fashionable and yet she is, and yesterday she indeed began to comprehend that she is in fact a European, who out of a sense of profundity all the more colorfully imagined for being actually absent, once laughingly turned down a proposal of marriage that was in itself rather romantic.

"Am I nothing but what I am?" she asked abruptly.

"You're a European. All Europeans without exception have hitherto made the incidentally quite understandable error of considering themselves to be far more than in truth they are," I replied.

Forgiving me for the information I had imparted, she betook herself off, as she had a call to pay.

With regard to prettiness and its absence, beautiful women are perhaps too self-preoccupied for purposes of Europeanness and may not have time to pursue so time-consuming a business as Europeanism with all its obligations.

Beauty is a form of power; power makes its possessor happy, while happiness requires nurturing and wishes to be in charge. Perhaps only those who serve can succeed in being European.

Autumn (II)

Little clouds that look like bits of cotton wool are drifting before my windowpanes in the yellow blue. I speak these last words with the indolence of a divinely gifted layabout, but let me add that a letter is lying in my manuscript holder that I shall possibly respond to. A different letter, that is, one whose contents struck me as unacceptably naïve, was out of laziness allowed to sail into the wastepaper basket. Frequently persons approach me with what I find the quite odd presumption of sharing with me this or that piece of advice which I am for the most part not at all inclined to heed. Along with the autumn season, the theater season arrived, as well as a magazine posing the question of what qualities must be displayed by a novel worthy of immortality.

With a sluggishness that is only to a certain extent ungraspable, I shall concern myself in the present deliberations with a sort of beggar who is whiling away his days in a very beautiful landscape and residing in a—to all appearances—magnificent house where he takes his coffee at four in the afternoon, after which he sets out to perform his habitual obligations. When he goes for a stroll, he finds himself encircled and en-ring-around-the-rosied by children, which fills him with disconcertions that arise possibly because of his inability to find much or anything at all within himself by way of innocuousness, despite his efforts on that score.

In earlier days, as he himself once related, he dwelt in a little

Microscript 72

103

castle whose graceful gable work was mirrored with poetical delicacy in the lake on whose atmospheric strand that residence stood. This beggar cannot be referred to as a needy petitioner meekly requesting, say, a bit of bread, but rather in discussing him one must speak of a spiritual beggarhood, which in and of itself is surely not so dire a circumstance, since the main thing for us when we have enough to eat is to know where we can go at night to rest from the day's exertions that deplete our strength. One thinks it permissible to voice the opinion that around the figure of the beggar it was autumn, whereby, however, error can by no means be ruled out. For example, I do not know with any certainty whether writers are authorized to compare the early morning with springtime, noon with summer, eventide with autumn and the long, monotonous hours of night with the winter season. Around the beggar, then, evening had arrived. Deep furrows nested on either side of his mouth, which could be seen as evidence that he was often at odds with himself.

At times he thought himself a magician. But whereas in former days he'd worked his magic with a sureness of hand, i.e., naïvely, as if playing upon the flute of the wealth of his unconscious, which is possibly a somewhat unquotidian way of putting it, now his spells suggested more a niggling hesitancy than a joyous striding forth into the reaches of Life. You insult Nature, in my opinion, if you impute, say, ill humor of some sort to the autumnal, since autumn takes umbrage at all admittedly tempting attempts to impose on it some affinity, as it were, with melancholy or beggardom; though to be sure it does sometimes seem that little autumnal trees can be found to harmonize with beggarly little faces.

The beggar was seated in a dainty pose upon a bench in the autumnal park, thinking about the letters he had addressed to the mistresses of his velvet black-soft heart, all of whom felt apprehensive on account of his magical beggarliness: "When he writes to me, might he be intending these lines for another?" is a question each had asked herself on being informed of his feelings of intimacy, and each of them had found it compelling to be propelled back and forth upon the swing of a tenderly tumescent disbelief. To a certain extent, the beggar had taken care to provide, in this respect, the most stimulating possible backdrop of naturalistic romanticism, which can be classed as a problem. Being himself so wary of belief, he had no choice but to render others doubtful as well when he put himself in their hands epistolarily, causing them to hearken to his manner of speaking. His way of loving, which was in a sense perhaps a little bit alarming, was often excused with reference to his not unpeculiar nature and its golden-sphere-like qualities, which kept rolling down the slopes of his existence. Anything false about him appeared to them to resound with openness, for this seeker, they thought, could only seek in his one-track way, just looking at his mirthfully earnest eyes revealed that at bottom he was plotting only to conjure up faithfulness from a soul—possibly at times a bit too zealously.

The beggar was constantly taking his autumnalities for granted, as though there were such a thing as precisely nuanced gradations of life.

It amuses me to believe that readers are, as it were, writers' chaperones; but even the most rigorous thinker may well have arrived perhaps at the surely capital insight that these lines of mine are autumnally fading—with which, in point of fact, their purpose has been fulfilled.

In the city where I reside, a Van Gogh exhibition is currently on view.

REDAKTION

DES

BERLINER TAGEBLATT

Sehr geehrter Herr
lauben,dass ich mir
kleinen Arbeiten hi
baren Raume darüber
netürlich eine gewi
so möchte ich alles
schickt haben,hier
Mit bester Empfehlu

A Sort of Cleopatra

Not having learned all too much with regard to herself in the course of her not particularly numerous experiences, she proceeded to acquire, on the basis of an income piling up as if playfully or jestingly, a household which featured silver and gold forks, knives and soup spoons and also leafy plants and a number of sofa pillows, and then from here it was a mere trifle for her imagination—beginning suddenly to awaken or grow active after having slept or reposed perhaps for days or even weeks—to instill in her the peacock-feather-fluttering illusion, gliding gently past as if upon a river in a boat bedecked with garlands, that she was a sort of Cleopatra longing for viper bites.

Entwined by hours of occupationlessness, she sometimes believed in a rather desultory fashion that she might possibly be making the discovery that she was in fact a boy who would gladly have seen himself transformed into a beautiful, delicate-limbed girl, or that, on the other hand, she was nothing more lowly or lofty than a girl growing up in a reformatory interlaced with principles—and therefore of necessity vigorously interlarded with rapscalities and the like—and constantly peering into life with its innumerable unfathomednesses or incalculabilities.

Given all this, no other ascertainedness could constitute the single correct factuality that prompted this modern-day Cleopatra to press from time to time, using her long, slender, pliant hand, a

Microscript 107

bell button, whereupon an utterly, that is, extremely solemnly clad gentleman finding himself in the so-called prime of life and lending confirmation to the highly obvious circumstance that he was indeed her lawful husband would enter the quite apposite room that distinguished itself by a certain luxuriousness of appointment, so as to suffer himself to be beseeched by a better half perhaps casually contemplating at such moments some thoroughly happenstance matter: "Please be so good as to betake yourself elsewhere at once, for I wish to behold before me a suitable convincing specimen, and this, as has no doubt been clear to you for some time now, you are not."

One fine day the painter Hans Makart, who was living in Munich, took upon himself with more or less dilatory speed or lightning-swift non-briskness the task of producing a painting—later to be covered with numerous cracks—whose figuration was based on this fascinating motif that is presently causing me to tremble with worry and the fear that I might prove incapable of making it my own, and which once drew, among others, a relatively successful British poet into its enchanting spell, if I may avail myself of a possibly somewhat too sonorous way of speaking.

Slaves one might at a moment's notice have made shorter by a head's length or who might just as easily in the twinkling of an eye become something quite respect-worthy, as was the case in the milieu where the original dwelt, were something which this epigone—to her disadvantage as well as, surely, her advantage—did not possess, though she was forced to ponder again and again whether or not she might be too precious and valuable to experience what is known as love.

Neither Caesars nor Antoniusses were prepared, it seemed, to have the benevolence and kindness to appear before her indubitably quite marvelous commanding visage.

What was going by the name of man generally struck her on the occasion of various events and opportunities as intolerably nugatory.

All those present-day kisses failed to possess in sufficient measure the instantaneously smoldering inflammation and flaming incandescence she longed for.

Melting beneath the non-sicklied-o'er pressure of an authenticity-laden kiss was denied her.

Her splendid skin, her muscles and veins, in short her complete organism, seemed ever incapable of partaking of the experience of that which the possesser of all these enumerated properties so dearly wished for.

Often she wished to wish for nothing at all.

She appeared capable of loving neither anything other than herself nor exclusively her own person, and the snakes of that Cleopatra who'd come before never slithered into the vicinity of her successor.

What use is it to take as one's example a paragon beyond one's reach?

Recently my eyes

Recently my eyes, reposing here upon Greek granite houses, read a clown essay penned as earnestly as you please. Imprecisely printed lines, I might add, have come to my attention, and while sampling a newspaper article I was struck by the catchphrase "building bridges." Let there ring out resoundingly into the wide world the following avowal: Scallywag Publishers has informed me of its willingness to respond to a portion of my impertinent demands regarding its blatant disgracefulnesses. Splendid, the way my poetical hand flies across the writing paper as if it bore a resemblance to a passionate dancer. Not one of my colleagues—and I am conscious here of speaking with comprehensive graspability—would succeed in putting forth so arresting a comment as now jubilantly proclaims: "Jesus was a Greek." Where might I have found the courage to venture such a claim? Thus do erudite observers of the theater long for salutary clownish mirth, and many whose duty it is to instill in young children a notion of life reach out their hands to grasp after Hellenic beauties. I hesitate not for an instant to inform the salons that in one of our papers that signify the culture of the age, a primary school teacher attacked his secondary counterpart with as ruthful a ruthlessness as his intellect commanded. I spent some time on holiday, where as a lover of Grecian lands I was permitted to study youthful equine limbs and the figures of lofty clouds, and while I now go on vehemently authoring

Microscript 12

away, a significant female personage is giving a Hellenic lecture in the auditorium of a school for elegant young ladies, and this woman is someone I know and esteem, apropos of which it occurs to me that I once read in a classic work the following note: "Never would the Greek theater have developed so vividly and vibrantly had not women kept away from it altogether." A German poet who was not in every respect happy wrote these words in a state of disgruntlement that might well be deemed regrettable. I for my part now write with undisguised clownish humor: "Socrates the Greek once, hoping to arrive via [...] at a clearer understanding of his own person, drank poison, and Diogenes too chose a protracted sojourn in a barrel over all other lifestyles, which may be taken as evidence that the Greeks did at times struggle with their own natures, that they did not always and everywhere love themselves and find themselves beautiful, as we contemporaries like to [...]". The author of the clown essay deserves recognition in my view because he takes seriously the good cheer that stems from immediacy. I am just reading a book by a celebrated novelist who cold-bloodedly antagonized yet another celebrated novelist by one day writing him a letter that accused him of having a "sycophantic soul." In truth he merely envied him his open, carefree mode of artistic production. "Simplemindedness, how I adore you," I might think myself entitled to cry out joyously with respect to Greece. The marble-cold statues of women encircled by the green of meadows and a flock's dingling bells will surely not be denied my undoubtedly worshipful admiration, and to the woman lecturer I duly expressed my thanks for her efforts aimed at portraying how in Greece plays were more frequently penned than epics and the like. Reading lets me travel in spirit, as I might permit myself in passing to append, and as soon as I have literarily amassed the cost of my passage, I shall depart with all possible haste to the land where stands a mountain yclept Olympus so as to breakfast high aloft in the company of all my having-made-it-thus-farnesses. If I meanwhile speak up in favor of female military service, it will perhaps sound odd, but in my opinion this can be seen as none other than a Grecian expression of views, though the Greek maidens of yore were more wont to sit daintily and delicately at home, wreathed about with zither-playing maidservants, upon the tumescent cushions of refined luxury. The longing for clowns appears to be identical with an appetite for something somehow bucolic; and as for the desire for all things Greek, there was once, not long ago, a Swiss writer by the name of Keller who mocked this propensity with an almost all-too Swiss, in other words bourgeois, sensibility. The aforementioned lout shall receive before day's end a message from me to the effect that his determination schools my poetic raptness, and those eyes the Greek women had, their wonderfully intertwining hair and the elegant staircases, free of even the tiniest grains of dust, that they ascended so as to enter the holy temples, my goodness, imagining all this classicism, all these splendidly erected societal structures and radiant resplendence robs me of the breath I would require to say anything more about the most significance-laden object that has ever set me in contemplative motion. I congratulate myself on having treated of a topic such as this, one about which I have no doubt said too little and which bids me murmur: "Done." What it means to cultivate pretensions on the basis of Greek prerequisites was experienced by no lesser light than Hölderlin, a bourgeois driven to bohemianism by bourgeois life, whose handsome if obstreperous figure allows me to be certain to believe that the mania for the Attic is, from the perspective of *bon ton*, all the same an educational and suitable pastime. In any reconstruction, it is always only what is pleasing that emerges, while that which genuinely existed eludes demonstration.

The words I'd like to utter

The words I'd like to utter here have a will of their own, they are stronger and more powerful than I am, and it seems to me as if they choose to sleep, or as if it pleases them not to be what they are, as if they find their idiosyncrasies too little diverting, and it does me no good to awaken them; my request: "Get up!" elicits no response at all, and naturally I myself find it both ingenious and exceptionally lovely the way I am refusing to recognize my words, as it were, indeed not even allowing them to recognize themselves, and as I stepped like this onto the pale, mountainous plain, I felt no desire to acknowledge myself as the one I was; instead I found it more sophisticated to persuade myself I was some Mr. So-and-so, just pulling from his pocket the realization that he is completely unrecognizable. While all who encountered me kindly acknowledged my lack of recognition, I inhaled with great relish something I would call "air" if I might possibly find it appropriate to dignify this substance filling my chest with a mention. [...] traversed the landscape of my own particularity—which I cannot call my own—like some utterly nameless Something, or perhaps the way a woman in her petticoats might enter a ballroom around the brilliantly illuminated midnight hour, when all good people, who at times can also be a wee bit bad, are living in the most longitudinal manner that exists, namely in bed. Stretched out to my full length, I ran with loudly resounding taciturnity across the unsheathed knives that tickled and kissed my foot-soles, provided it is not more fitting to stress that beneath my steps they compliantly curved. Knife: oh, what a loud, naïve, artless, simpleminded expression. Does not every word in and of itself signify an indiscretion, every *I* an impertinence? The absent ground on which I motionlessly walked compelled me at not a single instant to believe in it. Ineffabilities that I might describe quite well if this struck me as opportune tower up before my eyes, which deserve to be gouged out at once because they did not balk at having a name put to them. Beauty repulsive to look upon, decades-old centennial millennialisms in the most shapeless of shapes desired to have my blindness cast an eye on them. Hereupon I retrieved several small children from amid the multiplicity of my being and, beneath the professorial oversight I suddenly embody, did not [allow them] to play at all, for if I reported myself to be playing, it might offend the academic impulse within me. Horses and cows, to which I ought never thus to have given full-throatedly inadmissible voice, did something or other and appeared to busy themselves with an occupation that, if you insist, may be denominated eating grass. The face of the world resembled the visage of an offended woman who appeared to be in the most frightful apprehension over whether a person might under any circumstances be allowed to appear to be intending to display a feeling. Annoyance might turn out to be more appropriate than committing the incautiousness of loving while at the same time being filled with mortal hate. Suffused with venom, I cheerily remained the picture of good health; and while radiating ugliness, I embodied the certainty that I was the unshakable faça[de] of the most magnificent building, which is how my ramshackle benevolence understood itself. Each cow wore a bell at its neck, and every mountain range or ridge peered over the shoulder of its neighbor, and within all these muted surrounds the jingling of the little bells now leapt orchestrally about like sober jesters whose inaudibility was most clearly perceived, their visibility nowhere heard. With unassailable freedom of preach I now arrive in a position to say that now and then one of the grazing cows licked her spine or with enchanting sinuosities of tail whipped or thrashed the peacefulness and sweetness of the ground, and does not this poem composed in my bourgeois bedroom—for a poem I do consider it—not in the end merely represent an effort to call forth a bit of earnestness in those who will endeavor in vain to grasp this link in the chain of my prosaic writings, who consider themselves far too clever and are [in]capable of retaining their composure in the face of a tiny bit of foolishness, who have not yet even mastered the art of ignorance, who to this day have still not realized that they distinguish themselves by a glorious dearth of ideas, who often are not afraid of practicing decency in a colossally indecent manner, who know nothing of the birth of the understanding, nor of the beautiful wish that it not come properly to life, and who will scarcely be convinced by the odd and perhaps not entirely uninteresting attempt that has been made here to say something—anything—by means of these utterly meaningless remarks and to dispel all judiciousness as though this attempt were a sort of melancholy: one dreamed up by Dürer perhaps, laying her hand upon a globe. I can assure you that I found it extraordinarily difficult to behave with such frivolity. As if I didn't know the meaning of *bon ton*, but does anything of note ever result from it these days? Gazing upon my day's business, I began, as it were, with something heroic and then was glad to return to reason, and the flighty commencement was more difficult than finding my way, which came about really of its own accord. It's so easy not to err. Cleaving fast to what is proper and seemly can surely, all the same, be seen as a sort of laziness. How dumbfoundedly he now looks at me, the one who admonished me, with a reasonably suitable mien of inculpability, that I should be so good as to look after myself for once, as though he too were not adorned with something he had not managed, in all his life, to bring himself to follow: a fancy. Never once had he told a fib, and how sorry this makes him, and all this while he knows how very well I know him. How often he has withheld from me his applause, in bad conscience. He is torn, you see, and has always treated me as if I did not possess the intelligence to be at odds with myself. But now I've proven it.

The failure to prize the chance

The failure to prize the chance to spend time in a cosmopolitan city highly enough to refrain from giving it up in favor of an upstart one-horse town. Friends whispered into his metropolitan ear: "You'll be a fool if you don't set off at once for this backwater. Each and every inhabitant of this clod-and-furrow municipality (well furnished with nice places to go for a stroll) is awaiting your immediate arrival, the thought of which fills them with genuine pleasure." "Are you telling me this would be an opportune moment to swap metropolis for hamlet?" asked the problematic character. "Yes," they replied in chorus, whereupon he prepared himself for the journey with an alacrity utterly in keeping with his rural longings. With incomparable uprightness he resolved to become an honest cobbler or farmer. All at once he struck himself as so problematic as to be in every respect in need of repair, and while he sat in the railway carriage he thought of the beauty that lies in solidity and the solidness of beauty. His friends had doltishly sent telegraphic inquiries to the charmingly situated hamlet as to whether the moment was opportune for the arrival of their protégé, and the representatives of respectability had wired back with surprising speed: "Why, of course!" Privately, however, they were saying: "We'll show him a thing or two." Might he in fact have made a miscalculation concerning the character of this small town? Meadows, fields, trees, houses, the town gates, streets and street urchins—as

Microscript 419

all these neatly enumerated objectivities watched him ingenuously, trustingly approach—smiled. Straightaway they were seized by the far from pleasant feeling: "He is impertinent, and why? Because he has faith in our uprightness. And for what reason is his trust in us clodhoppers so boundless? Because he doesn't take us terribly seriously. He assumes we are simpletons one and all. Shall we demonstrate to this shiny, spiritual, well-travelled fellow that he has misjudged us? Yes—that's what we'll do." After they had reached an agreement on this score, they asked him: "Do you consider this an opportune moment to join forces with us?" "Yes," he replied. Hearing this guileless, incautious reply, they started laughing and said: "In that case, you would appear always to have taken us quite seriously. It turns out that you have posed yourself all sorts of questions on our account. To convince you of our fickleness, that is, of the fact that we are not entirely without intelligence, we declare to you that you have made on us the impression that you don't deserve that this moment might be opportune for you to endear yourself to us. You turned up here—because you were waiting with the utmost caution for a sign of our favor—at the most inopportune possible moment, and so we are informing you that we hold you, on account of your upright longing to become our esteemed fellow citizen, in contempt. We thought you were strong, and now you stand as a weakling before our eyes, which mock you." And in fact this is just how matters stood. I hope that many a deracinated soul will take a lesson from this essay and acknowledge that putting down roots is not so easily done. Besides which, people the least bit considerate of the need to preserve the orderliness of things are more likely to court disfavor than favor.

Herrn

Robert Walser.

Waldau.

As I was instructed by a book

As I was instructed by a book given me by a young lady who now and then was kind enough to inquire about my wellbeing, a good woman once had a bad husband. She was delicate, and he trivial. All her niceties had been entrusted to him one fine day for safe-keeping, as it were, and yet as the circumstances demonstrated, he had either no idea whatsoever or else very little notion of how to treat a tender soul. She shivered with cold in his bare, substandard presence, even lying in bed. Bed is derived from bad, how could a person fail to comprehend this. As long as she was single, she harbored only sweet, cheerful thoughts. Unimpeded, she was permitted to be a charming, attractive little idealist. But now, alas, things stood quite differently. Her husband's behavior regularly left her dumbstruck. Not a word occurred to her. She had the impression his uncouth presence was making her unintelligent, gradually sapping the ideas from her head. When she nonetheless managed some pronouncement, it was uttered in a tentative, lisping voice, which made it look as if she didn't know anything. In him, how-ever, people saw a run-of-the-mill individual, one of the many who set out in pursuit of nothing other than the earning of money (in and of itself quite a nice undertaking). Neglected, she sat for entire mornings and afternoons upon the sofa, and life seemed to her like a little ditty whose last notes fade away before it even begins. With a taken-for-grantedness that left nothing to be desired, he

Microscript 47

abandoned her to her unfulfilled assumptions. To the extent that he was unassuming, she was anything but. She was longing for something. It took her many days to come to a realization on this account. Finally it dawned on her that she wished to become bad, she no longer wanted to be pure, good and lovely. Being bad would undoubtedly be far simpler, easier and more effortless than playing a solid, refined role. Being good regardless of the circumstances— oh, how difficult this was proving to be. And so she ran out of the house into the street. The wind whistled, plucking at the trees, rain slapped against her cheeks, lights were shimmering in the dark. She ran through the black of night and soon vanished into one of those bars that imply ugly assumptions about ladies who set foot in them. For propriety's sake, let me leave her for the time being and content myself with expressing the wish that she return from this outing or detour into the unsavory realm of the sickly in the best of health. And indeed this is just what came to pass a short time later. I see her, to my satisfaction—though to be sure she is still somewhat haggard and suffers from all sorts of memories flicking about like will-o-the-wisps—breathing sighs of relief as she sits in a confidence-inspiring garret room. A man who showed understanding for her errant ways and was at pains to cheer her took her pale hand gently in his and coaxed from her a weak smile with his attempts at courtesy. She found herself well looked after. Once more she became good. This was no doubt what the course of things allowed and required of her.

Schnapps

Years ago I read a story treating of this topic in which a scholar who, finding himself displaced to flattish or hilly, sibilantly natural and rural surrounds and possessing, moreover, not much of a notion about how to come to terms with himself and his personal peculiarities, nearly shriveled up with odium. The peacefulness that confronted him at every turn, no matter where he looked or placed his foot, struck him as unendurable. He sat upon a settee whereupon already his grandfather had quite possibly stretched out in comfort's name. In vain did he entrust himself hopefully to this tasteful heirloom. Reading all sorts of apparently excellent books made him yawn. Imperceptibly he began to hit the bottle. But then a female acquaintanceship opening out blossomlike before him—inasmuch as he met a ravishing little damsel who inhabited a nearby estate and whose delicate-skinned hand he received permission to covet—lent his existence new, undreamed-of life pinions.

He realized that salvation was near.

If I may quote myself, I believe I am correct in recalling that around the time when I was still boyishly attending junior high school with an aim to filling myself with classical contextuality, I had a schoolmate whose father, a man who occasionally gathered wood in the forest, devoted himself on a daily basis to tippling, which was in no way advantageous to his son.

"To get schnappsed" is a jocular expression hereabouts meaning to receive a reprimand.

What a lovely, thrilling impression a cinematic schnapps scene of excellent quality made one day upon my spectating imagination.

A marvelously handsome young ethicist spoke enlighteningly with the populace, calling on it with ingenious eloquence to turn its back on schnapps once and for all. As he combated this intoxicant, however, he was himself paying tribute to it, distinguishing himself in the consumption of that very thing he was abjuring with spark-emitting zeal, and when asked why he was participating in the practice of that which he was at such pains to avoid or eradicate in principle, he replied that he was most convincing as an orator when in his cups, and that he found this contradiction enchanting.

Here too a lady made her appearance on the scene, his betrothed, to be precise, who addressed these words to the one whom in general she worshipped:

"Cut out the boozing!"

Never shall I forget the kind expression with which she framed her so earnest request.

And with this, my possibly somewhat unusual essay that nonetheless strives to fulfill insofar as possible the demands made by delicacy while at the same time aiming at solidity—containing as it does some words of warning—can no doubt be deemed to have come to an end.

Import englischer Stoffe

HANS MARTY

Burgdorf

Telephon 89

Vertreten durch: ....

New Year's Page

Year rhymes with hear, appear. Someone tapped at my door, I shouted "come in" and then hid in the wardrobe, and the one arriving no doubt stood listening, waiting for quite some time. Many a novel has begun in a promising way. Last night in a dream, my hands were transformed into rotten, crumbling towers. A ruin, I mean to say an aging millionairess, once bequeathed to me one hundred thousand francs, which in short order I squandered. What a beguiling memory! Back then, when I would step out of a place of entertainment into the fresh air of the street, the perspectives had a fairy-tale quality to them. There's no doubt something happy-making about spending money. I hope I shall soon succeed in penning a story that ought to be written as though a mandolin were being plucked. In the aforementioned dream my hands bellowed soundlessly for help. A bearlike groan shaggily lumbering from my lips awakened me, and I thought of a girl who had prophesied during my hundred thousand franc period that a time would come when I would be given the opportunity to heave deep sighs. Might I already have begun to approach a turning point of this sort? I am of good cheer in this regard, and shall come once more to speak of the dream whose events seemed intent on grinding me beneath their feet. Leafing through a newspaper as a young boy, I one day caught sight of an illustration depicting the chastisement of a slave. I'm being tapped on the shoulder by the question

Microscript 389

129

of whether I am at present writing quietly or loudly; by the same token I ask myself whether the present sketch sounds pointy or dull. In my opinion it sounds as if it were being dreamed up by a virtuous, reliable lout. The abovementioned wealthy woman incidentally displayed a highly expressive ugliness which was by no means a definitive deterrent for me. I once fell, on the occasion of an opportunity that presented itself, upon my knees before the figure she embodied, conduct that swayed or compelled this good woman, who had a reputation for wickedness, to consider me an exceptionally agreeable person. Assuming I do not lie, she wept with joy, although quite possibly she did so for some other reason. The girl who foretold a dire future for me wept herself one afternoon with sunlight shimmering all about her. During these proceedings I naturally had a hideously bad conscience. An overcoat from my champagne days can still be found in my possession. Somewhere or other a group of defenders of the fatherland were bunking down one chilly night; a nun with an unspeakably lovely face gave a pear to one of the soldiers who were constituting a pleasant-looking dispersion, selecting the one who among all of them appeared the least prepossessing; and the soldier in question possessed no gentility whatever, while the bestower or blesser was made of the loveliest decorum. This on the whole not terribly weighty experiencelet struck me as peculiar, for which reason it then, as it were, impressed itself on me as if forever. May I now devote my attention to a rapscallion who frightened his sensitive Mama by means of a ne'er-do-wellishness? Fear raced through her interiorities much like a horde of Huns who, according to world history, sped and dashed through the Europe of Early Medieviality. Some time ago in a field near our city, a horseshoe dating back to the age of the Huns was found and then incorporated into the historical museum. Inspiring fear can be described as a solecism based on lack of constraint.

Already twice in succession now the glory of the Nobel Prize in Literature has alighted on a female head.

One night, by the way, I felt a leathery, villainous hand touching my face. This terrifying experience imparted to me a fear that was Mont-Blanc-like in its monumentality.

I can't seem to resist the thought that at present we frequently have opportunity to read about crises and the like. Apparently it is practically a matter of *bon ton* nowadays to find oneself in a crisis of some sort.

How lovely the Christmas season was a few years ago. I walked silently through the streets, the ringing bells and silvery snowflakes. The casual manner in which I loved my beloved, who was forever distinguishing herself by her utter absence, resembled a soft-swelling, enchanting sofa. A much-loved authoress was at just this time delighting her followers with a charming new book. New Year's? Don't the words almost smell a bit like wistfulness? When a year stops, another instantly commences, as if one were turning the page. The story keeps on going, and the beauty of a context is revealed.

ABOUT THE MICROSCRIPTS

Each microscript facsimile included in this volume is followed by its translation or in the case of microscripts that contain multiple texts (as with Number Nine), by multiple translations, although we do not always translate all the texts on a given microscript. All facsimiles accompanying the English translations are reproduced at actual size. Many of the microscripts contain writing on both sides of the page; wherever this is the case, both sides are shown. If only one side is reproduced, the microscript contains no writing on the reverse.

The numbering system used to identify the microscripts has no relation to the date of composition. The microscripts were assigned their numbers in 1967 by Walser's editor Jochen Greven using a numbering system that reflects the (apparently random) order in which the texts were preserved by Walser's guardian Carl Seelig—at the time it was not obvious that it might some day be possible to date these works. Indeed, many of the dates assigned to the microscripts by their transcribers Bernhard Echte and Werner Morlang on the basis of contextual clues are approximate or speculative.

Most microscripts contain more than one text, including poems and "dramolettes" (short plays or dialogues), as well as the stories Walser himself tended to refer to as "Prosastücke" (prose pieces). The selection in this book concentrates on the stories and story fragments.

Walser did not generally title his microscripts, so they are referred to by their first lines. Some of the texts included in this volume do have titles; these are texts Walser copied over for submission to publishers. Some of these were published in newspapers at the time, though by this stage of Walser's career he was able to publish only a small percentage of the stories he produced.

The titled stories in this collection were translated from *Das Gesamtwerk*, edited by Jochen Greven (Frankfurt am Main: Suhrkamp, 1978). All others are from *Aus dem Bleistiftgebiet*, edited by Bernhard Echte and Werner Morlang (Frankfurt am Main: Suhrkamp, 1985–2000). Bracketed ellipses in the text indicate points where a word or passage was indecipherable or where the text breaks off.

Microscript 131 (page 6)
A poem and a prose text written on an envelope sent to Walser from the Rowohlt publishing house in Berlin on April 13, 1926.

Microscript 337 (pages 23–24)
Written between May and June 1926 on a sheet from a tear-off calendar. This story was published in the May 27, 1928, issue of the newspaper *Prager Presse*. Röbi is a Swiss diminutive for Robert.

Microscript 39 (pages 27–28)
In 1926 and 1927 Walser wrote a number of texts on the pages of the 1926 Tusculum weekly calendar published by Heimeran Verlag in Munich; he cut each page in half before writing on it. In all, 157 of these halved pages survive, including all

the pages of the calendar itself and many of the accompanying illustrations. This text, written on half of the calendar page for July 4–10, is thought to date from November or December 1926.

Microscript 200 (pages 33–34)
Written presumably in the fall of 1928 on a slip of paper cut from a magazine page.

Microscript 9 (pages 37–38)
Written in June or July 1932 on a card received from Eduard Korrodi, literature editor at the newspaper *Neue Zürcher Zeitung*, who writes to inform Walser that he is accepting two prose texts for publication. Walser prepared a fair copy of the second half of the first text reproduced here (beginning with the words "This tender bud led a precious existence…"), giving it the title "The Precious One," but it is not known to have been published.

Microscript 350 (page 52)
Written between October and December 1928 on part of an honorarium notice from Rudolf Mosse Verlag, publishers of the newspaper *Berliner Tageblatt*. This microscript contains a number of poems that Walser scratched out so thoroughly that even he would have been unable to read them. He also turned the final "G" of "Verlag" (publisher) into a "C" and added an "H" to make the end of the word spell out "ach" (a lament).

Microscript 54 (pages 55–56)
This is one of a number of microscripts dated simply 1930–1933, meaning that it was written during the period of Walser's voluntary residence in the Waldau Sanitarium in Bern before he was transferred against his will to the mental hospital in Herisau. It was written on the back of the torn-off front cover of a penny dreadful (*After the Torment*) and appears to have been inspired by the story of this book. Over the years, Walser wrote a large number of pieces that incorporated the sensationalistic plots of cheap romances.

Microscript 408 (pages 59–60)
Written between November and December 1927 on part of a postal wrapper from a periodical mailed in Prague. "The Prodigal Son" was published in the September 12, 1928, issue of the newspaper *Berliner Tageblatt*. The vertical ticks on the the text to produce a manuscript that could be submitted to publishers. *Glünggi* is a colorful Swiss-German insult that might translate as "idiot." Ernst Zahn (1867–1952) was a popular folksy Swiss author who set his sentimental tales in mountain or peasant milieus.

Microscript 190 (page 66)
Written between March and April 1925, this is one of the 117 microscripts written on sheets of the white paper used for art prints. Twenty-four such pages contain Walser's 1925 novel *The Robber*.

Microscript 23 (pages 71–72)
For the story "A Drive" (Autofahrt), published in *Berliner Tageblatt* on May 10, 1928,

Walser combined texts from two separate microscripts, 23 and 407a/I. Microscript 23, written on a halved calendar page (Aug. 15–21, 1926), contains the frame tale, while microscript 407a, written on part of a receipt for an honorarium issued by *Berliner Tageblatt* on Nov. 21, 1927, contains the inserted story "Teacher and Pastor" along with eight poems. Microscript 23 is believed to have been written during the summer of 1927, while microscript 407 dates from November or December of that year.

Microscript 407a/I (pages 73–74)
See *Microscript 23* above.

Microscript 50 (pages 79–80)
Written in 1930–33 on a strip of paper cut from the August 8, 1929, issue of the glossy lifestyle periodical *Sport im Bild*. The word "forging" in "farming and forging" might also have been transcribed as "tailoring." Walser's playful etymology notwithstanding, *Cheib* is actually a Swiss-German word, signifying, approximately, "jackass."

Microscript 215 (page 84)
Written between October and November 1928 on thin paper, glossy on one side. The narrator's startling the "refined individual" by shouting "Catch!" recalls a traumatic scene from Walser's 1907 novel *The Tanners* in which protagonist Simon Tanner's older brother Kaspar hurls a plate of sauerkraut across the dinner table with this imperative.

Microscript 116 (pages 89–90)
Written in December 1928, this text begins on the back of the publisher's card and continues on the front. Walser doctored the original card, apparently sent to him along with a copy of a novel by Max Brod (better known as Franz Kafka's confidant and literary executor), making it read, "Sent with compliments of ~~the author~~ poor Maxie." He replaced the name of the publisher, Zsolnay, with "Ränferli," an epithet no one to date has been able to explain. The address becomes "Little Fool Street" (based on the Swiss insult "Gigel"), and he adds the remarks: "The wicked Walser boys are always annoying one" and "published by Magical Publishing." Max Brod apparently once offered to talk to Zsolnay about printing some of Walser's work. In a letter to Brod dated October 4, 1927, Walser expresses skepticism about this possibility, writing that Zsolnay "runs like a rabbit before the outrageous suggestion that he might print, i.e., publish, poems."

Microscript 434 (pages 97–98)
Written between January and March 1928 on a strip of paper cut from the January 6, 1928, edition of *Sport im Bild*, this story was published in the March 28, 1928, issue of *Berliner Tageblatt*.

Microscript 72 (page 102)
Written on part of a postal wrapper in September 1927, this story appeared in the October 8, 1927, edition of *Berliner Tageblatt*.

Microscript 107 (page 106)
Written between September and November 1928 on part of a business letter from Fred Hildenbrand, on *Berliner Tageblatt* stationery, dated September 11, 1928. Austrian artist Hans Makart (1840–1884) painted a *Death of Cleopatra* that corresponds roughly to the scene here described. The "relatively successful British poet" here referred to may well be Shakespeare (*Anthony and Cleopatra*), given the Hamlet allusion later in the piece, though it might also be George Bernard Shaw, whose comedy *Caesar and Cleopatra* appeared in German translation in 1904.

Microscript 12 (page 110)
These two stories, written on a halved calendar page (Aug. 15–28, 1926), date from June or July 1927.

Microscript 419 (page 118)
Written probably during the winter of 1927–28 on a piece cut from an envelope.

Microscript 47 (page 122)
Written 1930–33 on part of an envelope sent to Walser at the Waldau Sanitarium. In the first text on this microscript, the phrase "ladies who set foot in them" might also have been transcribed "those who set foot in them."

Microscript 389 (pages 127–28)
Written in December 1928 or January 1929 on the business card of a gentleman who specialized in importing English fabrics.

Robert Walser

Walter Benjamin

We can read much by Robert Walser, but nothing about him. What in fact do we know about the few people among us who are able to take the cheap satirical gloss[1] in the right way—in other words, who do not behave like the hack who tries to ennoble it by "elevating" it to his own level? For the real challenge is to take advantage of the contemptible, unassuming potential of this form to create something which is alive and has a purifying effect. Few people understand this "minor genre," as Alfred Polgar[2] termed it, or realize how many butterflies of hope are repelled by the insolent, rocklike façade of so-called great literature, seeking refuge instead in its unpretentious calyxes. And others never guess the extent of their debt to a Polgar, a Hessel,[3] or a Walser for the many tender or prickly blooms that flourish in the barren wastes of the journalistic forests. In fact, the name Robert Walser is the last that would occur to them. For the first impulse of their meager store of cultural knowledge—their sole asset in literary matters—tells them that what they regard as the complete insignificance of content has to be compensated for by their "cultivated," "refined" attention to form. And in this respect what we find in Robert Walser is a neglect of style that is quite extraordinary and that is also hard to define. For the idea that this insignificant content could be important and

Walter Benjamin manuscript 797 *Layouts of Perception*

that this chaotic scatteredness could be a sign of stamina is the last thing that would occur to the casual observer of Walser's writings.

They are not easy to grasp. For we are accustomed to ponder the mysteries of style through the contemplation of more or less elaborate, fully intended works of art, whereas here we find ourselves confronted by a seemingly quite unintentional, but attractive, even fascinating, linguistic wilderness. And by a self-indulgence that covers the entire spectrum from gracefulness to bitterness. Seemingly unintentional, we said. Critics have sometimes disagreed about whether this is really so. But it is a fruitless quarrel, as we perceive when we recall Walser's admission that he never corrected a single line in his writing. We do not have to believe this, but would be well advised to do so. For we can set our minds at rest by realizing that to write yet never correct what has been written implies both the absence of intention and the most fully considered intentionality.

So far so good. But this cannot prevent us from trying to get to the bottom of this neglect of style. We have already asserted that his neglect makes use of every conceivable form. We should now add: with a single exception. And this exception is one of the most common sort—namely, one in which only content and nothing else counts. Walser is so little concerned with the way in which he writes that everything other than what he has to say recedes into the background. We could claim that what he has to say is exhausted in the process. This calls for explanation. And further investigation alerts us to a very Swiss feature of Walser's writing: his reticence [*Scham*]. The following story has been told of Arnold Böcklin, his son Carlo, and Gottfried Keller.[4] One day they were sitting in an inn, as they frequently did. Their regular table was well known for the taciturn, reserved habits of the drinking companions. On this occasion the group sat together in silence. The young Böcklin finally broke the lengthy silence with the words, "It's hot"; and after a further quarter of an hour had passed, his father added, "And there's no wind." As for Keller, he waited for a while, but finally got up and left, saying, "I won't drink with chatterboxes." The peasant linguistic reticence [*Sprachscham*] that is captured in this eccentric joke is typical of Walser. Scarcely has he taken up his pen than he is overwhelmed by a mood of desperation. Everything seems to be on the verge of disaster; a torrent of words pours from him in which the only point of every sentence is to make the reader forget the previous one. When in the course of a virtuoso piece he transforms Schiller's monologue "Along this narrow pathway must he come" into prose, he begins with the classic words, "Along this narrow pathway." But then his Wilhelm Tell is overcome by self-doubt, appears weak, insignificant, lost. He continues, "Along this narrow pathway must he come, I think."[5]

No doubt, such writing has its precedents. This chaste, artful clumsiness in all linguistic matters is heir to a tradition of folly. If Polonius, the model for all windbags, is a juggler, then Walser is a Bacchus who wreathes himself in linguistic garlands that then trip him up. The garland is in fact the proper image for his sentences. But the idea that stumbles around in them is a thief, a vagabond and genius—like the heroes of his writings. He is unable, incidentally, to depict anyone who is not a "hero"; he cannot free himself from his main characters and has contented himself with three early novels so that he can henceforth consort exclusively with his hundred favorite rascals.[6]

It is well known that the Germanic languages are particularly rich in heroes who are windbags, wastrels, and thieves, and who in general have gone to the dogs. Knut Hamsun, a master of such characters, has recently been discovered and celebrated. Eichendorff who created his Ne'er-do-well and Hebel his Firebrand Fred are others.[7] How do Walser's characters fare in such company?

And where do they spring from? We know where Eichendorff's Ne'er-do-well comes from: he comes from the woods and dales of Romantic Germany. Firebrand Fred comes from the rebellious, enlightened petty bourgeoisie of the Rhenish cities around the turn of the nineteenth century. Hamsun's characters come from the primeval world of the fjords—they are drawn to the trolls by their homesickness. And Walser's? Perhaps from the Glarn Alps? Or the meadows of Appenzell, where he hails from? Far from it. They come from the night at its blackest—a Venetian night, if you will, illuminated by the faint lamps of hope—with a little of the party spirit shining in their eyes, but distraught and sad to the point of tears. The tears they shed are his prose. For sobbing is the melody of Walser's loquaciousness. It reveals to us where his favorite characters come from—namely, from insanity and nowhere else. They are figures who have left madness behind them, and this is why they are marked by such a consistently heartrending, inhuman superficiality. If we were to attempt to sum up in a single phrase the delightful yet also uncanny element in them, we would have to say: *they have all been healed.* Admittedly, we are never shown this process of healing, unless we venture to approach his "Schneewittchen" [Snow White], one of the profoundest products of modern literature, and one which is enough on its own to explain why this seemingly most fanciful of all writers should have been a favorite author of the inexorable Franz Kafka.

These tales are quite extraordinarily delicate—everyone realizes that. But not everyone notices that they are the product not of the nervous tension of the decadent, but of the pure and vibrant mood of a convalescent. "I am horrified by the thought that I might attain worldly success," he says, in a paraphrase of Franz Moor's speech.[8] All his heroes share this horror. But why? Not from horror of the world, moral resentment, or pathos, but for wholly Epicurean reasons. They wish to enjoy themselves, and in this respect they display a quite exceptional ingenuity. Furthermore, they also display a quite exceptional nobility. And a quite exceptional legitimacy. For no one enjoys like a convalescent. The enjoyment of the convalescent has nothing of the orgy about it. His reinvigorated blood courses toward him from mountain streams, and the purer breath on his lips flows down from the treetops. Walser's characters share this childlike nobility with the characters in fairy tales, who likewise emerge from the night and from madness—namely, from the madness of myth. It is commonly thought that this process of awakening took place in the positive religions. If that is the case, it did not do so in any very straightforward or unambiguous way. The latter has to be sought in that great profane debate with myth that the fairy tale represents. Of course, fairy-tale characters are not like Walser's in any simple manner. They are still struggling to free themselves from their sufferings. Walser begins where the fairy tales stop. "And if they have not died, they live there still." Walser shows *how* they live. His writings—and with this I shall finish, as he begins—are called stories, essays, poetic works, short prose pieces, and the like.

Originally published in *Das Tagebuch*, September 1929.
Translated by Rodney Livingstone.

Benjamin published his essay on Walser in 1929, the same year that Walser entered Waldau Sanitarium. He had no knowledge of Walser's microscript method.

NOTES

1. The satirical gloss is a recognized literary form in German, more familiar than in English, where the term "gloss" refers mainly either to the interlinear gloss of medieval texts or to marginal comments of the kind Coleridge provides in "The Ancient Mariner." In German the gloss was developed into high art by Karl Kraus, who practiced it throughout his career in his commentaries on other writers and journalists in his periodical *Die Fackel.*

2. Alfred Polgar (1873–1955) was a Viennese journalist and a gifted literary critic and commentator on cultural trends. Many of his essays were collected and published in book form during his lifetime. He was famous for his elegant, ironic style.

3. Franz Hessel was a close friend of Benjamin and had worked with him both on the translation of Proust's *A la recherche du temps perdu* and in the early stages of Benjamin's *Passagen-werk* (Arcades Project). For Benjamin's evaluation of Hessel's importance, see "The Return of the *Flâneur*" and "Review of Hessel's *Heimliches Berlin,*" both in *Walter Benjamin: Selected Writings, Volume 2, 1927–1934* (Harvard University Press).

4. Arnold Böcklin (1827–1901), the Swiss painter, was known for his Romantic treatment of mythological subjects. Gottfried Keller (1819–1890), also Swiss, was the major exponent of literary realism in German. See Benjamin's essay "Gottfried Keller" in *Walter Benjamin: Selected Writings, Volume 2, 1927–1934.*

5. The quotation comes from the classic monologue in Schiller's *Wilhelm Tell,* Act 4, Scene 3. As Tell lies in wait for the tyrant Gessler, he reflects on the moral justification of the murder he is about to commit.

6. The three novels are *Geschwister Tanner* (The Tanners, 1907), *Der Gehülfe* (The Assistant, 1908), which is his best-known work, and *Jakob von Gunten* (1909).

7. Knut Hamsun (1859–1952) was a Norwegian novelist who criticized the American way of life and idealized the farmer's existence. He supported the German invasion of Norway and in 1947 was condemned for treason. His most famous— and extremely popular—novel was *Hunger* (1890). Joseph von Eichendorff (1788–1857) was one of the leading figures of German Romanticism. Known mainly for his lyric poetry, he also wrote the classic novella *Aus dem Leben eines Taugenichts* (Adventures of a Ne'er-do-well, 1826). Johann Peter Hebel (1760– 1826) was a journalist and author; he was much esteemed for the use of dialect in his writings, a practice that had fallen prey to eighteenth-century enlightened universalism. As editor and chief writer of the *Badischer Landkalendar,* an annual publication not unlike the American *Old Farmer's Almanac,* Hebel produced an enormous volume of prose and poetry. A typical calendar would include a cosmology embellished with anecdotes and stories, practical advice for the homeowner and farmer, reports on crime and catastrophe, short biographies, riddles, and, finally, political observations on the year just past. Hebel's narrative persona, the "Rhenish Family-Friend," narrates and comments; Sterne-like ironic interjections are not infrequent. See Benjamin's essays on

Hebel in Volume 1 of *Walter Benjamin: Selected Writings, Volume 1, 1913–1926* (Harvard University Press).
8. Franz Moor is the villain in Schiller's play *Die Räuber* (The Robbers).

Walter Benjamin Manuscript 797 (page 136)
Translated by Esther Leslie.

Layouts of Perception
In summer, one notices more the deep shadows, in winter the bright light.
In summer, fat people are conspicuous, in the winter the thin are.
In spring, attention is caught, in bright sunshine, by the young foliage, in cold rain, by the still leafless branches.
Inhabitants' most intimate sense of home in a town (indeed maybe also in the memory of the traveler who stays there a while) is connected with the sound and intermittence that the beat of its town clocks marks out.
What lends an incomparable tone to the very first view of a village or a town in the landscape is the fact that in one's image of it distance resonates just as importantly as nearness. This latter still has not yet gained preponderance through the constant exploration that has become habit. Once we begin to find our way around the place, that earliest picture can never be restored.

(The sense of touch does not teach us about the limits of what touches (the finger) but the touched (the object) Dr. Mannheim.)

Treading in two different ways: to touch one point of the earth—to touch the earth at one point. The first type is ours. When one sees Gothic decoration, one knows that older epochs possessed the second form.

On distant trees one sees not leaves but foliage.

He, who, awake and dressed, perhaps while hiking, witnesses the sunrise, preserves all day before others the serenity of one invisibly crowned, and he who sees daybreak while working feels at midday as if he himself has placed the crown upon his head. This same hour, its first early dawning is a moment of deep cleansing for those who are gathered—to bathe in the dawn's red is not a metaphor—for the freshly blemished, though, it is a judgment that announces itself internally.

143

Some Thoughts on Robert Walser

by Maira Kalman

A packKage aRRives.

It is Tied with Linen
and wRapped with a page
fRom a newspapeR. TheRe is
a photo of a man lying
dead
in the snow.

I am hoping that he is not
Dead, just enjoying a Refreshing
Lie-down in the snow. But the
caption, sadly, says he is Dead.

The man is Robert Walser,
the writeR. One of his Books
was JAKOB von GuntEn.
It tells the story of a boy who
attends the Benjamenta Institute
to become a seRvant in a gRand home.

Walser too, worked as a Butler, in this Grand but forbidding Silesian home. He also worked as an assistant to an inventor.

These two sisters
were kind to Walser,
encouraging his writing.
t things unraveled

and he started moving, from
one Rooming House to another.

How many corridors did he
walk down to how many Rooms?

How many times did he
Pack and Unpack suitcases?

How many wallpapers?
How many Beds?

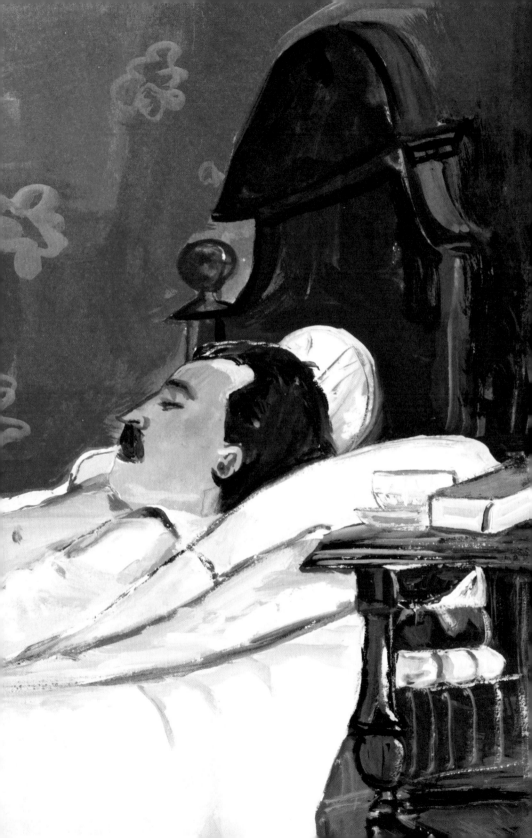

Lieber Robert Walser
who loved to walk so much. There
you are standing erect in a shabby suit.
Living so many years in a mental institution.

But allowed to take walks. Writing in
minuscule type with a stubby pencil.
But then saying "I'm not here to write, but to be mad.
And finally taking a walk on Christmas Day,
and dying in the snow. Perhaps not a
bad way to die. With your hat flown off your head

Acknowledgments

We would like to thank Reto Sorg, Lucas Marco Gisi, and the staff of the Robert Walser-Zentrum, Bern, for all they have done to make this project possible; Magnus Wieland of the Swiss Literary Archives, Bern; Margit Gigerl for her help in the initial stages and Jochen Greven for his patient answers to dozens of questions; Pro Helvetia and the Looren Translation House for providing support for the translation; the National Endowment for the Humanities; Petra Hardt and Suhrkamp Verlag; Rudolf and Eliane Stauch; Erdmut Wizisa, Oliver Kunisch and the Walter Benjamin Archiv; Breon Mitchell and the Lilly Library of Indiana University, Bloomington; and Monika Gadient and the *Neue Zürcher Zeitung*.

The Christine Burgin Gallery would like to thank Susan Bernofsky for her inspiring translations and for all her work and enthusiasm for this project; Maira Kalman for her love of Walser and her beautiful paintings and text; Laura Lindgren for the wonderful design and for sugggesting this project to Maira Kalman; Jason Burch for all his help; Barbara Epler and everyone at New Directions; Charlotte Sheedy, Jay Stewart at Capital Offset, and finally and especially, Jim Bibo and William Wegman.